Children's

Books

of

Yesterday

A Catalogue of an Exhibition
held at 7 Albemarle Street
London during May 1946
Compiled by Percy H. Mui
With a Foreword by
John Masefield

PUBLISHED FOR THE
NATIONAL BOOK LEAGUE BY
CAMBRIDGE UNIVERSITY PRESS

NOTE

The Council of the National Book League wishes to thank the National Magazine Company, Ltd., for the loan of the collection of children's books which forms the greater part of this Exhibition, and Mr. Percy H. Muir for arranging the Exhibition and preparing the catalogue. Thanks are also due to Messrs. Warne and Mr. K. W. G. Duke for the exhibits they have kindly lent

CAMBRIDGE
UNIVERSITY PRESS

University Printing House, Cambridge CB2 8BS, United Kingdom

Cambridge University Press is part of the University of Cambridge.

It furthers the University's mission by disseminating knowledge in the pursuit of education, learning and research at the highest international levels of excellence.

www.cambridge.org
Information on this title: www.cambridge.org/9781107487260

© Cambridge University Press 1946

First published 1946
Re-issued 2015

A catalogue record for this publication is available from the British Library

ISBN 978-1-107-48726-0 Paperback

Foreword

I am glad that the first peace-time Exhibition to be held by the National Book League, and the first in its own home, will be of books for children.

If children use books at all, it is for the marrow of enjoyment to be found in them. What they seek in books is delight. In their search for delight they often ignore the teaching which the cunning elder thought to impart when he wrote the book. The child may think that the powder of instruction only shows the author's failure to keep up the quality of jelly throughout his work.

The books here displayed should be of the deepest interest to the National Book League and to the nation. We do not now hold the view that "All Children are by Nature evil"; but we do believe that children, like adults, should be lured and coaxed into the use of books. Here are the devices which the genius of four centuries has invented to lure some dozen generations of the young into civility. Here are a thousand hints for coaxing the young of this world into a new humanity.

JOHN MASEFIELD

Introduction

Most of the books in this exhibition originally formed the collection of the late F. R. Bussell. They were sold at Sotheby's on February 3, 1945, and were purchased as a collection by Elkin Mathews Ltd. on behalf of the National Magazine Co., by whose courtesy they are now exhibited. The Beatrix Potter exhibit has been made possible by the generosity of her executors and of her publishers—Frederick Warne & Co., Ltd. The games, jig-saw puzzles, and peep-shows are from my own collection.

The lay-out and type design of the catalogue are the work of Mr. Robert Harling.

In preparing the catalogue I have referred to the following books :—

- F. J. Harvey Darton. *Children's Books in England.* Cambridge University Press, 1932.
- E. M. Field. *The Child and His Book.* Wells, Gardner, 1891.
- A. W. Tuer. *Pages and Pictures from Forgotten Children's Books.* Leadenhall Press, 1898-9.
- Gumuchian. *Les Livres de l'Enfance du XVe au XIXe Siecle.* 2 vols. Gumuchian et Cie. Paris, N.D.
- C. Welsh. *A Bookseller of the Last Century. Being some Account of the Life of John Newbery.* Griffith, Farran, etc., 1885.
- T. Hugo. *The Bewick Collector.* 2 vols. Reeve, 1866-68.
- A. S. W. Rosenbach. *Early American Children's Books.* Portland, Maine, 1933.

P. H. MUIR

PART I

Instructional

F. J. HARVEY DARTON begins his charming book on Children's Books* by defining terms :— ' By " Children's books " ' he writes, ' I mean printed works produced ostensibly to give children spontaneous pleasure, and not primarily to teach them, nor solely to make them good, nor to keep them *profitably* quiet.' To observe that Darton's own book, not to mention the major portion of the present exhibition, is an elaborate confutation of this definition is rendered superfluous by the qualifications with which Darton concludes his first paragraph—' The definition is given as a broad principle liable to perpetual exception.' Those who plough patiently through the books now exhibited may well conclude that the exceptions to his rule are too frequent to serve as proof of it, rather they call for its abandonment.

Darton's definition, in fact, misses the point that books are most frequently provided for children by their elders. Among the motives of these elders is undoubtedly " to give children spontaneous pleasure," but the motive of most parents is not single in this respect and surely one test of the suitability of their choice is that it shall keep the child quiet, although whether " profitably " or not is a secondary consideration.

* F. J. Harvey Darton. *Children's Books in England.* Cambridge University Press. 1932.

Be that as it may, unless the book consists wholly or mainly of pictures, it is useless to a child who cannot read. This must be sufficient excuse for the nature of this first section of our exhibition, which endeavours to show a skeleton of the history of instructional literature. We begin with

SECTION I: THE ALPHABET

An early form of which was the Horn-book. This consisted of a paper or vellum rectangle on which was printed the alphabet and a few simple words. This was laid down on a piece of wood, which was provided with a handle, and the lettering was protected by a sheet of transparent horn, similar to that used in early lanterns—or lanthorns. The method may have originated in the sixteenth century ; the earliest use of the word quoted in the Oxford Dictionary is from Shakespeare, *Love's Labour Lost*, 1589, but Mrs. Field* mentions the grant of a licence for a " Horne A B C " to John Wolfe in about 1587.

" Horn-books " were also made of pewter, in which the letters were punched, and also of silver with letters handsomely engraved. All early horn-books are exceedingly rare and genuine specimens are seldom met with outside museums. Most of those offered for sale nowadays are fakes. We have, therefore, had to content ourselves with a genuine specimen from the first quarter of the nineteenth century (see No. 1), of about the

---

* *The Child and His Book.*   Wells, Gardner, pp. 114-5.

6

time when horn-books were giving way to Battledores.

The name of Battledore is taken from the secondary use to which children put their horn-books. Our specimen of the latter is rather stylized, but earlier examples are in size and shape eminently suited and were inevitably converted into bats for shuttlecocks. We show two groups of Battledores of different periods (Nos. 2 and 3).

A B C's for children existed before horn-books, indeed, a few years ago a " parcel " of numerous copies of a single-sheet alphabet, printed in Leipzig in about 1544, was discovered in new condition—among the oldest " remainders " on record. The sheet was headed *Tabulae Abcdariae Pueriles*, and comprised three alphabets, a Tabula Syllabarum and the Paternoster. Even earlier than this alphabets had been introduced into breviaries, on which there is a note in the next sub-section, under " Primers."

Our range of alphabets is unambitious by comparison, extending no further back than the second half of the eighteenth century, but thenceforward it is representative of developments during the subsequent hundred years or so.

1 A HORN-BOOK OF THE FIRST QUARTER OF THE NINETEENTH CENTURY.

2 A SELECTION OF BATTLEDORES, *ca.* 1810-1825. Rusher of Banbury and Davison of Alnwick were noted publishers of chap-books for children. (See Part III, Section i).

3 A SELECTION OF BATTLEDORES OF A LATER PERIOD. *ca.* 1850. An apparently unsuccessful attempt to revive the method.

4 ALPHABETS. A SERIES OF FRENCH LESSON CARDS BEGINNING WITH ALPHABETS AND PROCEEDING THROUGH SYLLABLES AND SIMPLE WORDS TO GRADUATED READING LESSONS. [*18th century*].

5 THE ENIGMATICAL ALPHABET, OR TWENTY-FIVE PUZZLES FOR A CURIOUS BOY OR GIRL. *Salisbury* : *C. Fellows. London* : *J. Wallis.* [*ca.* 1790]. Puzzle verses, the answer to each being a letter of the alphabet. " J " is omitted in accordance with its synonymity with " I " in the minds of printers.

6 THE ALPHABET IN VERSE. *Darton & Harvey*, 1800.

7 A SET OF COLOURED FLOWERS AND THE ALPHABET FOR LITTLE CHILDREN. *Darton & Harvey*, 1800.

8 R. R. THE INVITED ALPHABET, OR ADDRESS OF A TO B, CONTAINING HIS FRIENDLY PROPOSAL FOR THE AMUSEMENT AND INSTRUCTION OF GOOD CHILDREN. *Darton*, 1808. With 26 engraved plates of the Alphabet, the central figures of which are demonstrating the deaf and dumb alphabet. The captions constitute a simple story in verse, the purpose of which is to invite the Alphabet to assemble so that good children may learn to spell and read.

9 R. R. THE ASSEMBLED ALPHABET ; OR ACCEPTANCE OF A'S INVITATION . . . BEING A SEQUEL TO THE " INVITED ALPHABET." *Darton*, 1813. A Sequel to the foregoing, in which the letters of the alphabet gather in " abcdary coalition " with the desired effect—or so the concluding verses assure us.

10   PICTURE ALPHABET.   *ca.* 1810.   This picture
      sheet appears to be a development of the
      Battledore.

11   ALPHABET (A COLOURED PICTORIAL).   *ca.* 1810
      Engraved throughout, with coloured frontis·
      piece, 26 coloured plates of the Alphabet on
      7 pages and 8 coloured plates of the story of
      an industrious apprentice.

12   THE AMUSING ALPHABET FOR YOUNG CHILDREN
      BEGINNING TO READ.   *Taylor*, 1812.   With
      25 full-page engravings and a story to each
      letter of the alphabet, the title of which
      begins with that letter.

13   THE HISTORICAL ALPHABET.   *Harris*, 1812.
      Engraved throughout with 26 full-page
      coloured plates of scenes from English
      History.

14   W. BELCH'S NEW AND AMUSING ALPHABET.
      ca. 1815.   Belch was an early recruit to the
      penny plain, twopence coloured school of
      publishing and issued juvenile dramas, tinsel
      pictures and the like.

15   THE MURRAY ALPHABET ; OR PLEASING PIC-
      TURES.   *Blake*, *ca.* 1815.   With 12 rather
      crudely coloured engravings.

16   CLASSICAL LETTERS, OR ALPHABET OF MEMORY ;
      INTENDED FOR THE INSTRUCTION AND AMUSE-
      MENT OF YOUNG GENTLEMEN.   *Harris*, 1817.
      With frontispiece and 23 full-page plates in
      colour.   An ambitious but unsuccessful
      attempt at erudition.

17   GOOD CHILD'S REWARD (THE), OR A SCRIP-
      TURAL ALPHABET IN VERSES FOR CHILDREN
      . . .   *Chelmsford* : *Marden*, *ca.* 1820.   Two
      illustrated alphabets, one with verses.

18 THE GALLOPING GUIDE TO THE A B C, OR THE CHILD'S AGREEABLE INTRODUCTION TO A KNOWLEDGE OF THE ALPHABET. *Banbury* : *Rusher, ca.* 1820. A penny chap-book alphabet.

19 MRS. LOVECHILD'S GOLDEN PRESENT, FOR ALL GOOD LITTLE BOYS AND GIRLS. *York* : *Kendrew, ca.* 1820. A common usage of the " Dame " notion so popular with publishers and effective with children.

20 AN ALPHABETICAL ARRANGEMENT OF ANIMALS FOR LITTLE NATURALISTS. BY SALLY SKETCH. *Harris*, 1821. A most charming A.B.C, engraved throughout, in colour, with frontispiece, title, and 26 plates.

21 FLORA'S ALPHABET : OR THE GOOD CHILD'S FLOWER GARDEN. *Hodgson*, 1822. With a coloured engraved title and 24 half-page coloured engravings of flowers.

22 THE LIFE AND DEATH OF AN APPLE-PIE. *Carvalho, ca.* 1825. One of the most favoured of all alphabets. There is a version by Kate Greenaway (See 723b) and the verses are still popular with modern children.

23 A B C. PETER PARLEY'S PRIMER, AND LADDER TO LEARNING, OR ALPHABET IN VERSE. *Lacey, ca.* 1835. With 24 coloured cuts, one to each letter of the alphabet. The original Peter Parley was Samuel Griswold Goodrich, born at Ridgefield, Connecticut, in 1793. He had at least six imitators in England, who assumed his popular pseudonym. Edward Lacey, publisher of the present volume, was one of the first.

24 OSBOURNE (CHARLES, JUN.). A PICTORIAL ALPHABET. *Osbourne and Ackermann*, 1840. With booklet of explanation, engraved title and 26 pretty engravings, each on a separate card and each a representation of a letter of the alphabet, in pictorial form.

25 ALPHABET (A FRENCH AND ENGLISH), IN PANORAMA FORM. *ca.* 1840. 25 plates and one on the cover.

26 THE ALPHABET OF EXCITEMENT. *Harwood, ca.* 1840. An alphabet in which the subjects are portrayed in the shape or attitude of letters. The plates are lithographic.

27 PAPA'S GIFT FOR A GOOD CHILD. *Johnson, ca.* 1840. Coloured woodcut title and pictorial alphabet.

28 A B C FOR THE NURSERY. *ca.* 1840. With 26 coloured woodcuts.

29 [A PICTORIAL ALPHABET]. *ca.* 1840. A single sheet folded to 8 pp., in colour.

30 THE MODERN PICTURE ALPHABET OF CURIOSITIES. *March, ca.* 1840. A picture alphabet and first reader

31 THE SPELLING BEE : A LETTERS-TRY GAME. *ca.* 1850. An early version of " Word-Taking and Word-Making," " Lexicon," etc. Observe the atrocious pun in the title.

32 PRINCE ARTHUR'S ALPHABET ; OR, A WAS AN ARCHER. *Dean, ca.* 1850. An ambitious and fairly successful " moveable."

33 [AN ALLITERATIVE ALPHABET IN PANORAMIC FORM. *ca.* 1850]. The perplexities of the letter X are not shirked.

34 THE NEW LONDON ALPHABET, in Rhyme, with 28 pictures of the Principal Places in that far-famed City. *Darton*, [*ca.* 1850].

34a DEAN'S STEAMBOAT ALPHABET. *ca.* 1850. This may be rolled off in panoramic form taking the reader through a journey by steamboat.

35 THE A B C OF ALL NATIONS. *ca.* 1860. Flat wooden blocks with a coloured pictorial alphabet on one side and plain block capitals on the other.

36 THE NURSERY LIBRARY ALPHABET. *Routledge*, *ca.* 1860. The complete " library " of twelve volumes progresses through A Spelling Book and A Reading Book, to Natural History, Games, and finally, " Hymns and Songs."

37 THE CHILD'S OWN ALPHABET AND OBJECT LESSONS. *Darton*, *ca.* 1860.

38 RAILWAY A.B.C. *Warne*, *ca.* 1865. Printed in oil colours by Kronheim & Co., who held a licence from George Baxter.

39 LES ALPHABETS AMUSANTS. No. 2. ALPHABET DU PETIT MARQUIS . . . *ca.* 1870. A French picture alphabet in panorama form.

40 THE NOAH'S ARK ALPHABET. *Routledge*, [1872]. An early example of the work of Walter Crane. Each picture is signed with the familiar rebus.

41 THE ALPHABET OF GAMES. *Warne*, *ca.* 1875.

42 TOM THUMB'S ALPHABET. Illustrated by W. McConnell. Engraved by the Brothers Dalziel. *Bogue*, *ca.* 1880.

SECTION II: THE THREE R's

(a) **Reading.** This section includes the earliest book in the exhibition, the first English translation of Calvin's " Catechism " (No. 43). There is ample evidence that the earliest reading books for children were works of religious instruction. A " Primer," or " Prymer," was originally a breviary, but in the latter half of the fourteenth century, before the invention of printing in the western world, Chaucer's reference in the Prioress' Tale to a child at school learning his letters from " his prymer " shows the use it commonly served. In about 1537 was published *The Primer in English most necessary for the education of children*, which included one leaf containing the A B C. The " Shorter Catechism " was the other favoured book for this purpose, and the title-page of Crespin's translation of Calvin leaves no shadow of doubt that his book was expressly intended for the instruction of children, although he may have considered reading merely incidental to salvation.

43 CALVIN (JOHN). THE CATECHISME OR MANNER TO TEACHE CHILDREN THE CHRISTIAN RELIGION, WHEREIN THE MINISTER DEMANDETH THE QUESTION, AND THE CHILDE MAKETH ANSWERE. MADE BY THE EXCELLENT DOCTOR AND PASTOR IN CHRISTES CHURCHE, JOHN CALVIN. [*Geneva*] *By John Crespin, 1556.* The first English translation of Calvin's Catechism. This was used not only to teach children their religious duties, but also as a reading book. It is the earliest book in the exhibition, only two other copies are recorded in the *Short Title Catalogue* of English Books printed before 1640, one in the British Museum and the other in the Bodleian Library.

44 FAMILIAR FORMES OF SPEAKING COMPOS'D FOR THE USE OF SCHOOLS, FORMERLY FITTED FOR THE EXERCISE OF A PRIVATE SCHOOL ONLY, NOW PUBLISHED FOR COMMON USE. PARTLY GATHERED, PARTLY COMPOSED. *Printed by J. R. for T. Helder*, 1678. This is as much a Latin primer as a reading book, but also serves the latter purpose.

45 REACH (B.). INSTRUCTIONS FOR CHILDREN OR THE CHILD'S AND YOUTH'S DELIGHT, TEACHING AN EASY WAY TO SPELL AND READ TRUE ENGLISH ... *Haw*, [*ca.* 1700]. The full title-page as exhibited shows the full scope of the book and the frontispiece its grim moral tone. Numeration, punctuation, weights and measures are also shortly touched upon.

46 [ERRINGTON (PRIDEAUX)]. NEW COPIES IN VERSE FOR THE USE OF WRITING-SCHOOLS : CONSISTING OF FIFTY-THREE ALPHABETS ... *Newcastle upon Tyne* : *Isaac Lane*, 1734. Each of the fifty-three verses consists of twenty-four lines, each line beginning with a different letter of the alphabet consecutively from A to Z, omitting J and V.

47 A SPELLING-DICTIONARY OF THE ENGLISH LANGUAGE, ON A NEW PLAN. FOR THE USE OF YOUNG GENTLEMEN, LADIES AND FOREIGN-ERS. BEING AN INTRODUCTORY PART OF THE CIRCLE OF SCIENCES ... THE SIXTH EDITION. *J. Newbery*, 1757. This was the third volume of a series of ten issued by Newbery as " The Circle of Sciences." The first volume was a

14

" Royal Battledore " of which all trace now appears to be lost ; the second was a Grammar, now (1757 above) incorporated in the " Spelling Dictionary." They were first issued in 1745 and formed Newbery's third venture after his arrival in London. Collins of Salisbury, his almost invariable partner in his earliest publications, seems to have taken no share in this one.

48 THE CHILD'S NEW PLAY-THING : BEING A SPELLING BOOK INTENDED TO MAKE THE LEARNING TO READ A DIVERSION INSTEAD OF A TASK . . . EIGHTH EDITION. *Ware, Hawes, etc.*, 1763. Originally published in 1749 this is the earliest reading-book, consciously designed as such, in the exhibition. The device of printing as a frontispiece the portrait of a youthful royal prince was intended to suggest patronage in high places which had no existence in fact.

49 TOM THUMB'S FOLIO ; OR A NEW PENNY PLAY-THING FOR LITTLE GIANTS, TO WHICH IS PREFIXED, AN ABSTRACT OF THE LIFE OF MR. THUMB . . . *Newbery and Carnan*, 1768. The only other copy of this first edition, recorded by Welsh in his book on the Newbery family, is in the Bodleian Library.

50 LADDER TO LEARNING (THE). STEP THE FIRST : BEING A COLLECTION OF SELECT FABLES, CONSISTING OF WORDS OF ONLY ONE SYLLABLE. (2) STEP THE SECOND : BEING A COLLECTION OF SELECT FABLES, WITH ORIGINAL MORALS, UPON A NEW PLAN. CONSISTING OF WORDS NOT EXCEEDING TWO SYLLABLES. (3) STEP THE THIRD : BEING A COLLECTION OF SELECT FABLES, INTENDED AS AN EASY INTRODUCTION TO THE USEFUL ART OF

READING. *E. Newbery*, [1789]. The complete series bound together in one volume. Welsh was unable to see these and quotes them only from Newbery's list.

51 NEW LONDON READING (THE), MADE COMPLETELY EASY ... *Evans*, [18th century].

52 SPELLING BOOK (A), DESIGNED TO RENDER THE ACQUISITION OF THE RUDIMENTS OF OUR NATIVE LANGUAGE EASY AND PLEASANT ... TO WHICH IS PREFIXED, THE CHILD'S LIBRARY ; OR A CATALOGUE OF BOOKS, RECOMMENDED TO CHILDREN FROM THE AGE OF THREE TO TWELVE YEARS. BY MRS. TEACHWELL. *Marshall*, [*ca.* 1790].

53 READING MADE MOST EASY ... BY W. RUSHER, BANBURY. *J. Rusher*, [*ca.* 1790].

54 FENNING (D.). THE UNIVERSAL SPELLING-BOOK ; OR, A NEW AND EASY GUIDE TO THE ENGLISH LANGUAGE ... *For the Booksellers*, 1793.

55 LESSONS FOR CHILDREN FROM TWO TO THREE YEARS OLD. *Johnson*, 1797. The idea of a " first reader " begins to take definite shape. There are no pictures.

56 MAVOR (WILLIAM). THE ENGLISH SPELLING BOOK ... *Phillips*, [1801]. Extremely scarce. One of the most famous and successful of spelling-books, afterwards illustrated by Kate Greenaway. The frontispiece is by Stothard.

57 SHORT STORIES, IN WORDS OF ONE SYLLABLE ; BY THE AUTHOR OF " SUMMER RAMBLES." *Lloyd*, 1801. The " first reader " acquires a frontispiece, but no other pictures. Edward Lloyd, the publisher of this volume, was better known for his Gothic " shockers."

58 COLLYER (JOHN). READING MADE EASY ...
BEGINNING WITH WORDS OF ONE SYLLABLE
... *Nottingham* : *Burbage and Stretton*,
1801.

58a THE INFANT'S TUTOR. *J. Bysh, ca.* 1805.
Thirty-eight coloured plates of simple objects
—an early picture-reading book.

59 READING MADE COMPLETELY EASY : ... FOR
THE USE OF SCHOOLS. BEING AN IMPROVE-
MENT OF DYKE, WEALD, ETC. *Crosby*, 1806.
Bewick's influence on children's books, as on
illustrated books of all kinds, was incalculable
and considerable. His versions of early
readers are included with his other books in
the Illustrated Section of the Exhibition
(Nos. 700 to 712). The present book is at
once an example of that influence and of
the dawning realization of the importance
of pictures in reading books. It has a
woodcut frontispiece, 3 other full-page cuts,
and 94 charming small cuts in the Bewick
manner.

60 AMUSING OBSERVATIONS PURPOSED TO BE
MADE BY CHILDREN IN EARLY LIFE, WHICH
WILL ENABLE THEM TO READ ... BY THE
AUTHOR OF ... " SUMMER RAMBLES," ETC.
Harris, 1808. The illustrated " first reader "
has now completely emerged with pictures
that really illustrate the text.

61 UNIVERSAL PRIMMER (THE) ; OR, CHILD'S FIRST
LESSON. *Congleton* : *Dean*, [*ca.* 1810]. Note
the spelling on the title-page, which indicates
the old pronunciation of " Primer."

62 THE SILVER PRIMER ; OR, FIRST BOOK FOR
CHILDREN. *York* : *Kendrew*, [*ca.* 1815]. A
pictorial alphabet and first reader.

17

63 THE RATIONAL PRIMER. *Darton,* 1816. An illustrated A B C and first reader. With 32 small woodcuts, four to a page.

64 DIALOGUES CONSISTING OF WORDS OF ONE SYLLABLE ONLY ; INTENDED AS A PROPER BOOK TO FOLLOW THE IMPERIAL PRIMER. BY THE AUTHOR OF " SUMMER RAMBLES," ETC. *Harris,* 1816.

65 SIX STORIES FOR THE NURSERY ; IN WORDS OF ONE OR TWO SYLLABLES. BY A MOTHER. *Godwin,* 1819.

66 A B C UND BILDER-BUCH. (NEU VERBES-SERTES). *Berlin : Hasselberg,* [*ca.* 1820]. A typical German production of the period.

67 THE OFFICER'S DAUGHTERS, OR EMILY AND KITTY ; IN WORDS OF THREE SYLLABLES. *Miller,* [*ca.* 1820]. With a coloured engraved frontispiece and title, and 4 full-page coloured plates. Hand-colouring, carried out by children, was commonly used in the cheapest books at this period.

68 MEEKE (MRS.). MAMMA'S GIFT ; OR, PLEASING LESSONS, ADAPTED FOR CHILDREN OF AN EARLY AGE. *Dean and Munday, ca.* 1820. A typical early production of the still famous producers of children's books. At this period they were closely associated with the firm of A. K. Newman & Co., " descendants " of the Minerva Press, and books are commonly found with the imprint of either firm. *Dame Wiggins of Lee* is the best-known example. (See No. 295).

69 FLETCHER (REV. W.). THE PICTURESQUE PRIMER ... *Harris, ca.* 1820. A most charming production, with 120 coloured pictures on 18 pages.

70 THE INFANT'S TOY BOOK. *Dean, ca.* 1825. With 16 half-page hand-coloured cuts. Munday's name is no longer in the imprint.

71 LESSONS ON COMMON THINGS FOR LITTLE CHILDREN. *Darton, ca.* 1825. An early example of what became a very popular kind of book, with 12 coloured plates illustrating some 150 common objects.

72 YOUTH'S GUIDE, ADAPTED TO THE USE OF SCHOOLS BY A GENTLEMAN. *Deal : Hayward,* 1829. Illustrated alphabet and numerous other cuts.

73 THE STORY OF LITTLE MARY AND HER CAT, IN WORDS NOT EXCEEDING TWO SYLLABLES. *Darton and Clark,* [1830]. Five full-page hand-coloured engravings.

73a EASY STORIES FOR THE AMUSEMENT AND INFORMATION OF CHILDREN OF FOUR AND FIVE YEARS OLD. *Hailes,* 1831.

74 MAMMA'S LESSONS FOR HER LITTLE BOYS AND GIRLS ... Sq. 12mo. *Harris,* 1835. With 16 full-page coloured engravings.

75 DILWORTH (T.). A NEW GUIDE TO THE ENGLISH TONGUE ... Sm. 4to. *Weston,* 1836.

76 HASTIE (T.). THE ONLY METHOD TO MAKE READING EASY ... 8vo. *Newcastle : Charnley,* 1839. The description on the title-page " Seventy-Third Edition," is probably no exaggeration, for the book was originally published in about 1775. The charming cuts by Bewick are remarkably well printed considering their age and frequent use.

77 BROWN'S ROYAL VICTORIA PRIMER ; OR, CHILD'S FIRST BOOK. 8vo. *Whittaker & Co.,* [1841]. The hideous frontispiece of the young Queen accords ill with the attempt to cash in on her popularity and to suggest, with the royal arms on the title-page, an entirely fictitious patronage.

78 KEBLE'S NEW PRIMER ; OR, READING MADE EASY. Sm. 8vo. *Margate* : *Printed and Published by the Editor,* [ca. 1845].

79 LITTLE STORIES OF ONE AND TWO SYLLABLES, FOR LITTLE CHILDREN. First edition, sq. 12mo. *Masters,* 1849. With 9 full-page coloured cuts.

80 HARRISON (WILLIAM). THE INFANTILE CLASS BOOK ; OR, EASY READING, ADAPTED FOR CLASSES. 12mo. *Bingley* : *J. Harrison & Son,* 1853.

(*b*) **Writing.** Learning to write calls into play a new activity on the child's part. Manual dexterity and some degree of coincidence between hand and eye are necessary to its accomplishment. Like reading, it is a basic necessity without which education cannot be pursued very far and it is, therefore, not surprising that an important by-product of the renaissance of learning should have been the new profession of writing-master, nor that the profession should have originated in Italy, and reached England by way of France. The first copy-book published in England was an adaptation by John Baildon of a French work by Jean de Beauchesne and it appeared in 1571. The interaction between pure learning and the commercial advantages of being able to write and cipher (the writing-masters soon added

arithmetic to their curriculum — *cf.* Cocker)
cannot be pursued here, neither can the process
by which the elegancies of the early scripts
degenerated into copperplate. The history of
the subject is most conveniently found in Sir
Ambrose Heal's *English Writing-masters*, Cambridge University Press, 1931.

We show specimens of books of instruction
from the seventeenth, eighteenth, and nineteenth
centuries, and a number of writing-sheets. These
writing-sheets, or " school-pieces," were extremely
popular from about 1740 to 1850. They were
bought by children for a few pence, the centre-
space was filled in in the child's best handwriting
and presented to the parents usually at
Christmastide.

The immediate derivation of these sheets
from the copy-books of the period is well illustrated by the early examples shewn. This is
especially obvious in Nos. 87, 90 and 91, but all
the eighteenth century examples shew the same
influence very clearly.

81 SPECIMEN SHEETS FROM THE ORIGINAL EDITION
OF MARTIN BILLINGSLEY'S *The Pen's Excel-
lencie*, 1618. Shewing the variety and
elegance of the calligraphy of the time.

82 SHELLEY (GEORGE). ALPHABETS, IN ALL THE
HANDS ... Oblong 4to. *Overton*, [1710].
Shelley was one of the most famous of writing-
masters, and officiated at Christ's Hospital.
It is clear from this book that nearly all the
earlier styles of calligraphy were still taught
at this time. The title-page is an early effort
at calligraphic engraving by a member of
the Bickham family.

83 A GUIDE FOR THE CHILD AND YOUTH. IN TWO PARTS. THE FIRST FOR CHILDREN ... THE SECOND FOR YOUTH. TEACHING TO WRITE, CAST ACCOUNT, AND READ MORE PERFECTLY. BY T. H., M.A., TEACHER OF A PRIVATE SCHOOL. First edition, 16mo. 1725. *Printed by J. Roberts for the Company of Stationers.* There are four plates of copies in this book, three of which are varieties of copperplate. The book appears to be extremely rare and is not recorded in Heal's " Writing-masters."

84 SCOTT (ROBERT). THE PRINCIPLES OF WRITING DELINEATED AND EXEMPLIFIED ... First edition, 8vo. *Edinburgh : Bell & Bradfute, etc.,* 1820. The beginning of the dreary pot-hooks of our own youth. This, like many of the earlier works on the subject, has a section on how to make quill pens.

WRITING SHEETS OR SCHOOL-PIECES :—

85 THE SEQUEL OF THE LIFE AND FABLES OF AESOP. *James Cole, Engraver. April* 17*th,* 1741.

86 [INCIDENTS IN THE LIFE OF JESUS]. *T. Wilson, [ca.* 1749]. A most interesting example from many points of view. Note that the publisher is son-in-law and successor (a very common form of business succession) to the late James Cole (publisher of the previous sheet) where 104 of these sheets were already available. The cherubs in the corners are typical examples of calligraphic virtuosity, and so is the motto " Vive la Plume." The dating of the handwritten part at Christmas shews that from the beginning these sheets were used as Christmas greetings to parents and are thus forerunners of the Christmas card.

87 THE ALPHABET. *Sold by Robert Sayer*, [*ca.* 1750]. Sayer was a prolific publisher of engravings of all kinds. He took over, successively, the firms of Philip and Henry Overton, whose father, John, had founded the business in the seventeenth century. Sayer was in turn succeeded by Laurie & Whittle. (See below).

88 THE FLAMES OF WAR BREAKING OUT IN GERMANY. *Sold by Joseph Hawkins, September 12th, 1757*. Hawkins, like Cole, was a prolific publisher of these sheets. He published two sequels to this one, the first on the exploits of Frederick the Great, the second is No. 89 in this catalogue.

89 THE BLESSINGS OF PEACE AND THE CALAMITIES OF WAR. *Sep.* 27, 1762. A Sequel to No. 88. Note that the handwritten part is dated at Christmas.

90 THE HEADS OF EM^T· ENGLISH MAST^RS· DEC^D· *Sold by Robert Sayer* [*after* 1763]. This and the next piece form a most direct link between the writing-masters and these sheets. The portraits are rough copies of frontispieces to books by these masters. The date is inferred from the inclusion of Abraham Nicholas, who died in 1763.

91 THE FIVE SENSES. *Sayer* [*before* 1765]. A rare example, unique in our experience, of a child's writing-sheet signed by a writing-master. James Champion, senior, died about 1765.

92 HISTORICAL EVENTS. *I. Farrell*, 1774.

93 THE VICISSITUDES OF FORTUNE, OR END OF HUMAN GLORY. *Josh. Hawkins, Junr., April 10th*, 1780.

94 [ALPHABET OF NATIONS]. *T. Farrell, April 20th*, 1787. A deliberate return to the calligraphic style. The figures, charming though they are, are almost subordinate to the flourished decoration. Note the naivety of the " Letter Y "—for which no nation could be found and the ingenious inclusion of " Otaheitan " and " Quaker." The " Otaheitan " and the " Zealander " were very topical in view of Cook's voyages of discovery.

95 VIRTUE TRIUMPHANT OVER VICE. *Laurie and Whittle*, 12th May, 1794. The paper on which this is printed is watermarked 1804, which shows the persistent popularity of old designs and also marks a pointer for the collector.

96 NAVAL AND MILITARY SCHOOL PIECE. *Bowles and Carver*, [ca. 1797].

97 TRADES ADAPTED TO THE CONVENIENCE AND HAPPINESS OF SOCIETY. *W. & T. Darton*, *August 12th*, 1808. The earliest writing-sheet we have seen with a Darton imprint : none are known to us with the imprint of the Gracechurch St. firm, of which the Holborn Hill shop was an offshoot.

98 THE FIRST GRAND ATTACK UPON FLUSHING, BY THE BRITISH FORCES. *Laurie & Whittle*, *9th Novr.*, 1809. Note the use of rockets as a munition of war.

99 HARLEQUIN AND MOTHER GOOSE : OR THE GOLDEN EGG. *Laurie & Whittle, March 25*, 1807. Compare this with the " Harlequinades," Nos. 816 to 834.

100 WATERLOO BRIDGE, AS IT APPEARED ON THE DAY OF OPENING, JUNE 18TH, 1817. *Jas. Whittle, and R. H. Laurie, 29th Octr.* 1817. Note the style in the change of the firm, the original Laurie has been succeeded by his son, and Whittle has become the senior partner.

101 KING HENRY THE 8TH. *W. Belch, etc.,* [*ca.* 1815]. The grace and delicate colouring of the early examples is beginning to disappear. It is significant that Belch was a prolific publisher of juvenile dramas of the " penny plain " school.

102 GUY FAWKES, OR THE GUN POWDER TREASON, NOVEMBER 5TH, 1605. *R. H. Laurie, 1st October,* 1823. Whittle has now disappeared and Laurie junior reigns alone. His productions retain a full share of the old elegance.

103 THE DEATH OF ANANIAS. *W. Belch and J. Phelps,* [*ca.* 1840]. The crudity of the printing contrasts strongly with the grace of the handwriting—the work of a boy of eleven !

(*c*) **Arithmetic.** The books shewn in this section of the exhibition are not purely educational ; they are intended rather to illustrate the ingenuity displayed in attempts to make instruction attractive to children. Early arithmetics for juveniles are mostly as dull as their modern counterparts, but the few items shewn in the present section are evidence of awareness that numeration and calculation appeal less universally to children than the two other R's.

104 JUVENILE IMPROVEMENT. ARITHMETIC. MULTIPLICATION TABLE, SET TO MUSIC BY I. W. CALLCOTT. Second edition. 1797.

105 AN ARITHMETICAL PASTIME, INTENDED TO INFUSE THE RUDIMENTS OF ARITHMETIC UNDER THE IDEA OF AMUSEMENT. *John Wallis*, 1798. The wording of the title betrays a probably all-too-well justified doubt that the " amusement " is overborne by the formidably obvious instructional nature of this " Pastime."

106 R. R. INFANTILE ERUDITION TO WHICH ARE ADDED THE FIGURE DANCERS. THE WHOLE INTENDED AS A SUPPLEMENT TO THE INVITED AND ASSEMBLED ALPHABETS. First edition, sq. 12mo. *Tabart*, 1810. The preface explains the principle as follows :—" These dancers are exhibited in the costume of Arabians, the reputed inventors of our modern arithmetical numeration ; the numbers are individually denoted by the ornaments in their turbans ; and the algebraic signs of the four principal rules by their attitudes,"which is all extremely ingenious, though its effectiveness is doubtful.

107 BELCH'S NURSERY CALCULATIONS, OR A PEEP INTO NUMBERS. First edition, sm. 8vo. *Belch*, [*ca*. 1815]. Less ingenious and probably equally ineffective.

108 MARMADUKE MULTIPLY'S MERRY METHOD OF MAKING MINOR MATHEMATICIANS ; OR THE MULTIPLICATION TABLE ILLUSTRATED. First edition, sq. 12mo. *Harris*, 1816. With 69 coloured engravings, with engraved text below each, going up to twelve times twelve on the rhyming principle.

109 NATHANIEL NUMERAL'S NOVEL NOTIONS OF ACQUIRING A KNOWLEDGE OF NUMERATION. First edition, sq. 12mo. *Wallis*, 1817. With 16 coloured engravings. Another attempt to teach the multiplication table by rhymes.

110 [PENCE TABLE]. First edition, sq. 12mo. *Harris*, 1818. A similar attempt to teach the coinage system.

111 THE NEW GAME OF THE PENCE TABLE. *D. Carvalho*, [1826]. Note the reference in the instructions to " Fishes " used as chips. These were the familiar bone, ivory, or mother-of-pearl fishes now frequently found in antique shops. The date of the game is taken from the watermark.

112 THE MULTIPLICATION TABLE IN VERSE. First edition, 8vo. *Wallis*, [ca. 1830].

113 A SELECTION OF PICTORIAL SHEETS USED FOR TEACHING THE RUDIMENTS OF ARITHMETIC. [ca. 1850-60]. Ingenuity seems here at last to be coupled with effectiveness in a simple way.

114 PERCY CRUIKSHANK'S COMIC MULTIPLICATION TABLE. *Read & Co.* [ca. 1865].

114a MULTIPLICATION TABLE NEATLY DISSECTED. [*No imprint*], ca. 1840. A pretty jig-saw which ingeniously contains the multiplication table in 35 pieces.

SECTION III : SPECIAL SUBJECTS

(a) Grammar and Punctuation.

115 THE CHILD'S GRAMMAR, DESIGNED TO ENABLE LADIES WHO MAY NOT HAVE ATTENDED TO THE SUBJECT THEMSELVES TO INSTRUCT THEIR CHILDREN. First edition, 12mo. *Marshall*, [ca. 1785]. The wording of the sub-title is commendable more for its frankness than for its selling power.

116 THE MOTHER'S GRAMMAR. BEING A CONTINU-
ATION OF THE CHILD'S GRAMMAR, WITH
LESSONS FOR PARSING ... First edition,
12mo. *Marshall*, [*ca*. 1790].

117 A GRAMMATICAL GAME IN RHYME. BY A
LADY. *Published for the Author by S. Conder*,
1802. Note the price—half a guinea—
probably equivalent to about three times as
much in modern currency.

118 MADAME LEINSTEIN. PUNCTUATION IN VERSE ;
OR, THE GOOD CHILD'S BOOK OF STOPS. *Dean
& Munday*, [*ca*. 1820]. First edition, 8vo.

119 MADAME LEINSTEIN. THE RUDIMENTS OF
GRAMMAR, IN VERSE ; OR, A PARTY TO THE
FAIR. First edition, 8vo. *Dean and Munday*,
[*ca*. 1820]. With a frontispiece of " Miss
Syntax's School," and 12 half-page illustra-
tions, all in colour.

120 PUNCTUATION PERSONIFIED : OR POINTING
MADE EASY. BY MR. STOPS. First edition,
8vo. *Harris*, [*ca*. 1820].

121 INFANT'S GRAMMAR, OR A PIC-NIC PARTY OF
THE PARTS OF SPEECH. First edition, 8vo.
Harris and Son, 1824.

122 PETER PIPER'S PRACTICAL PRINCIPLES OF
PLAIN AND PERFECT PRONUNCIATION. . . .
First edition, 8vo. *Harris*, 1822. This is
largely an alphabet with a charming coloured
woodcut to each letter and an alliterative
verse beneath, thus : " Andrew Airpump
ask'd his Aunt her Ailment . . . etc."

123 POPULAR ERRORS IN ENGLISH GRAMMAR,
PARTICULARLY IN PRONUNCIATION, FAMILI-
ARLY POINTED OUT ... 12mo. *Wilson*, 1827.

(b) Scripture.

124 AN HISTORY OF THE LIVES, ACTIONS, TRAVELS, SUFFERINGS, AND DEATHS OF THE MOST EMINENT MARTYRS, AND PRIMITIVE FATHERS OF THE CHURCH, IN THE FIRST FOUR CENTURIES. First edition, 16mo. *Newbery*, 1764. An extremely scarce little book, which is not recorded in Welsh's monograph on the Newberys.

125 MASON (W.). THE HISTORY OF JESUS; DRAWN UP FOR THE INSTRUCTION OF CHIL-DREN. 12mo. *Printed for the Author*, 1775.

125a WALLIS'S KEY TO THE OLD TESTAMENT. [*ca.* 1790]. A very eary jig-saw and one of the first to depart from the previously invariable " dissected map " type.

126 THE SINCERE CHRISTIAN'S DEVOUT COMPANION ... [*No place or publisher*], 1796. The popularity of tracts began in the second half of the eighteenth century. They were mainly distributed by chapmen and colporteurs.

127 A CONCISE HISTORY OF THE HOLY BIBLE. TO WHICH IS ADDED AN APPENDIX CONTAINING SEVERAL USEFUL CALCULATIONS, NEVER BEFORE PRINTED. First edition, 32mo. *Liverpool* : *T. Schofield*, 1799. The sub-title is a catchpenny, for the " appendix " contains nothing but a list of other books sold by Schofield.

128 THE HISTORY OF JOSEPH. COMPILED IN AN EASY AND FAMILIAR WAY, FOR THE ENTER-TAINMENT AND INSTRUCTION OF YOUTH. First edition, 12mo. *Coventry* : *Luckman & Suffield*, [*ca.* 1800]. Compare this with Nos. 130 and 133 for later treatments of the same subject.

129 SUNDAY READING. LOOK AT HOME; OR, THE ACCUSERS ACCUSED... *Sold by J. Marshall, etc.* [*ca.* 1800]. A typical example of the work of the Cheap Repository for whom many such tracts were written by Hannah More.

129a JOLLY (WILLIAM). MY BIBLE. *Darton*, 1812. An example of an uncommon type of jigsaw, adapted from a book. The book is based on the style of Ann Taylor's poem " My Mother," which had many imitators. Note the signed guarantee of perfection on the lid which was operative as long as the seal was unbroken.

130 THE HISTORY OF JOSEPH AND HIS BRETHREN ... *Paisley: Caldwell,* [*ca.* 1820]. Compare this with Nos. 128 and 133.

131 BETTS'S SCRIPTURAL PASTIME. NEW TESTAMENT. *John Betts,* 1837. Complete with the question cards, the key containing the answers and a map of Palestine to which some questions refer. The compiler confesses, in the preface to the key, to a reluctance to associate " Sacred History with anything bearing the semblance of a game " and only its suitability as a Sabbath pastime induced him to publish it.

132 FIFTY PICTORIAL ILLUSTRATIONS OF THE LORD. *Varty,* 1844.

133 HISTORY OF JOSEPH. *Darton & Hodge,* [*ca.* 1865]. Compare earlier treatments of the subject in Nos. 128 and 130.

(c) **History.**

With the teaching of history the opportunities for ingenuity increase enormously. The subjects hitherto under consideration do not lend themselves very readily to any treatment other than in book form. Scripture is an exception, but the compiler of No. 131 has already given us a hint of the danger of any attempt to relieve the serious, if not gloomy atmosphere, then considered indispensable to the subject. Such impiety was liable to a penalty of ostracism not encouraging to the enterprising publisher. The two jig-saw puzzles shown are other rare examples of attempts to alleviate the tedium of the nineteenth century Sabbath. The proper answer to the suggestion put forward in No. 131 that the Sabbath needed any alleviation was, of course, that it was impious to suggest the playing of games on the Sacred Day and there can be little doubt that there were references to that thin end of the wedge which has always been the standard weapon of English revolutionaries.

No such prohibition could be suggested with subjects proper to be studied only on week-days. Moreover, if children must be allowed to play games—and the young renegades seem to have insisted on doing so—by all means let them be as improving and instructive as possible. Hence the prevalence, throughout the earlier period of our exhibition, of such games as those in this section, by means of which the hours of leisure were made, as far as possible, extension of the hours of study.

134 NEWBERY (J.). A COMPENDIOUS HISTORY OF THE WORLD FROM THE CREATION TO YE DISSOLUTION OF THE ROMAN REPUBLIC, COMPILED FOR THE USE OF YOUNG GENTLEMEN AND LADIES BY THEIR OLD FRIEND MR. NEWBERY. VOL. I. First edition, 16mo. *For J. Newbery*, 1763. Extremely rare. The only reference to the book we can trace is Welsh's statement, p. 237, that Darton and Harvey produced an edition of it in 1804. Illustrated with engravings.

135 ACCOUNT OF THE CONSTITUTION AND PRESENT STATE OF GREAT BRITAIN, TOGETHER WITH A VIEW OF ITS TRADE, POLICY AND INTEREST, RESPECTING OTHER NATIONS ... *Newbery and Carnan*, [ca. 1765]. According to Welsh, p. 233, this book was originally published by John Newbery in 1759, but no copy of the first edition appears to be known.

136 A NEW HISTORY OF ENGLAND, FROM THE INVASION OF JULIUS CAESAR TO THE PRESENT TIME. ADORNED WITH CUTS OF ALL THE KINGS AND QUEENS WHO HAVE REIGNED SINCE THE NORMAN CONQUEST. 12mo. *Carnan and Newbery*, 1770. Welsh (p. 212) does not record this edition. The book was originally published by J. Newbery in 1761.

137 [COOPER (THE REV. S.)]. A NEW ROMAN HISTORY, FROM THE FOUNDATION OF ROME TO THE END OF THE COMMON-WEALTH ... DESIGNED FOR THE USE OF YOUNG LADIES AND GENTLEMEN. *E. Newbery*, 1784. This is the rare first edition of a book of which Welsh describes the edition of 1800 and knows of none earlier than 1789.

138 [COOPER (REV. MR.)]. THE HISTORY OF FRANCE FROM THE EARLIEST PERIOD TO THE PRESENT TIME ... First edition, sm. 8vo. *E. Newbery*, 1786.

139 THE LIVES OF THE BRITISH ADMIRALS, DISPLAYING, IN THE MOST STRIKING COLOURS, THE CONDUCT AND HEROISM OF THE NAVAL COMMANDERS OF GREAT BRITAIN AND IRELAND First edition, 2 vols., 16mo. *E. Newbery*, 1787. Extremely scarce, with 24 engraved portraits, two to a page.

140 TRIMMER (MRS. SARAH). DESCRIPTION OF A SET OF PRINTS ... First edition, 6 vols., sq. 12mo. *Marshall*, [*ca.* 1787-8]. A fine set of Mrs. Trimmer's famous " Descriptions." " The perusal in 1787 of Mme. de Genlis's ' Adèle et Théodore ' gave Mrs. Trimmer the idea of having prints engraved with subjects from sacred and profane history, to hang up in nurseries, accompanied by books of explanation ... The plan of teaching little children from pictures is now adopted in most infant schools."—*D.N.B.* Darton (p. 160) doubts the influence of Madame de Genlis on Mrs. Trimmer, but the wording on the author's own dedicatory letter in the " Scripture History "—the earliest of the series—leaves little doubt of her own sense of indebtedness to that lady.

This set comprises :—English History, 2 vols. ; Roman History and Ancient History, 2 vols. ; Scripture History and New Testament History, 2 vols.

141 CHOICE SCRAPS, HISTORICAL AND BIOGRAPHICAL, CONSISTING OF PLEASING STORIES AND DIVERTING ANECDOTES, MOST OF THEM SHORT TO PREVENT THEIR BEING TIRESOME, COMPRE-

HENDING MUCH USEFUL INFORMATION AND INNOCENT AMUSEMENT, FOR YOUNG MINDS. First edition, 12mo. *E. Newbery*, [1790 or '91]. Welsh, p. 183.

142 AN ACCOUNT OF THE ROYAL CASTLE AND CHAPEL OF ST. GEORGE IN WINDSOR. First edition, 12mo. *G. Thompson, and Champante and Whitrow*, [ca. 1799].

143 [GODWIN (WILLIAM)]. OUTLINES OF ENGLISH HISTORY. BY EDWARD BALDWIN. *Godwin*, 1808. In 1806 Mrs. Godwin published her husband's " History of England " for schools. The pseudonym of " Edward Baldwin " was adopted because Godwin's own name was too closely associated with heterodoxy to commend him to parents. The above abridgement was prepared by Godwin to appeal to a different public. We show the cover for its view of Mrs. Godwin's shop. (See also No. 144).

144 [GODWIN (W.)]. THE HISTORY OF ENGLAND, FOR THE USE OF SCHOOLS. BY EDWARD BALDWIN. *Godwin*, 1818. (See the note to No. 143).

145 BROWN (LOUISA). HISTORICAL QUESTIONS ON THE KINGS OF ENGLAND, IN VERSE. First edition, 12mo. 1813.

146 TAYLOR (REV. ISAAC). BEGINNINGS OF EUROPEAN BIOGRAPHY. THE EARLY AGES. ... First edition, 8vo. *Harris*, [ca. 1820]. For a note on the Taylor family see p. 94.

147 HISTORICAL PRINTS : REPRESENTING SOME OF THE MOST MEMORABLE EVENTS IN ENGLISH HISTORY. *Harvey and Darton*, [ca. 1820 ?].

147a PICTURES FROM GRECIAN HISTORY. *Darton,*
ca. 1820. A fine jig-saw.

148 BARBER (AGNES ANNE). ENTERTAINING
STORIES, IN VERSE, SELECTED FROM ENGLISH
HISTORY, ADAPTED FOR THE IMPROVEMENT
OF YOUNG PERSONS. First edition, sm. 8vo.
Thomas, etc., 1825:

149 THE BRITISH SOVEREIGNS, FROM WILLIAM THE
CONQUEROR TO VICTORIA THE FIRST. [*ca.*
1840]. Interesting comparisons may be
made between this sheet and the various
card-games (*e.g.* Nos. 151 and 154 and esp.
No. 163), and jig-saw puzzles (*e.g.* No. 152)
of a similar type.

150 THE PENNY HISTORY OF ENGLAND. *March,*
[*ca.* 1851]. The later history is treated in
the most tendencious manner, with distinct
leanings towards Chartism.

HISTORICAL GAMES :—

151 HISTORICAL CARDS EXHIBITING THE HISTORY
OF ENGLAND. *Wallis,* [*after* 1760]. Beginning
with William the Conqueror and ending with
the death of George II.

152 WALLIS'S ROYAL CHRONOLOGICAL TABLES OF
ENGLISH HISTORY ON A PLAN SIMILAR TO
THAT OF THE DISSECTED MAPS. *Wallis,*
March 31*st,* 1788. Begins with William the
Conqueror and ends with the death of
George II. Note that the sides of this jig-
saw puzzle are not straight—a common
feature of early examples.

153 THE ROYAL GENEALOGICAL PASTIME OF THE
SOVEREIGNS OF ENGLAND. FROM EGBERT TO
GEORGE THE 3RD. *E. Newbery & J. Wallis,*
Novr. 30*th,* 1791.

154 HISTORICAL PASTIME, OR A NEW GAME OF THE HISTORY OF ENGLAND, FROM THE CONQUEST TO THE ACCESSION OF GEORGE THE THIRD. *J. Harris & J. Wallis, Decr. 1st,* 1802. Compare this with No. 155.

155 HISTORICAL PASTIME ... *E. Wallis & J. Harris & Son, [after* 1830]. An excellent example of the way in which these games were adapted to bring them up to date may be seen by comparing this with No. 154. Note also the changes in the imprints of both publishers.

156 THE JUBILEE : A NEW AND INTERESTING GAME. *J. Harris, Jan. 1st,* 1810. Note the family likeness between this and, *e.g.,* Nos. 154 and 155.

157 INSTRUCTIVE CONVERSATION CARDS, CONSISTING OF 32 BIOGRAPHICAL SKETCHES OF EMINENT BRITISH CHARACTERS. *Darton, [ca.* 1810]. A question and answer game, with forfeits.

158 THE ROYAL GAME OF BRITISH SOVEREIGNS, EXHIBITING THE MOST REMARKABLE EVENTS IN EACH REIGN FROM EGBERT TO GEORGE III. *E. Wallis,* [1829]. We have placed this game out of strict chronological order because it is a re-issue of an original publication of 1814. The title-page to the book of " Explanation " calls it the fifth edition. The latest incident depicted on the " board " is Napoleon's departure for Elba on square 53 (1814). The " Explanation " includes his return to France (1815), and the date of the present " edition " as 1829.

159 THE ROYAL GAME OF BRITISH SOVEREIGNS . . . FROM EGBERT THE FIRST KING, TO THAT OF HIS PRESENT MAJESTY. *E. Wallis*, [*c.* 1837].

Another example of continued popularity, provided for by ingenious adaptation. Squares 1 to 52 on the " board " depict roughly the scenes as those in No. 158, although changes will be noted in many of the pictures. No. 53, however, has been curtailed leaving room for the depiction of one scene each from the reigns of GEORGE IV AND WILLIAM IV. From the wording of the title-page to the book of " Explanation " it seems that the game was issued in this form some time after 1830 when William acceded. The grand new centre-piece and an additional paragraph in the " Explanation " were all that was needed to restore topicality after the Queen's accession.

160 THE LIFE AND MILITARY ADVENTURES OF THE DUKE OF WELLINGTON . . . *D. Carvalho*, [*ca.* 1820].

161 PICTORIAL ILLUSTRATIONS OF ENGLISH HISTORY FROM THE DEATH OF RICHARD III TO WILLIAM THE FOURTH. *E. C. Edlin*, [*after* 1830].

161a THE INTERROGATORY GAME OF ROMAN HISTORY. *Betts*, 1836. A question and answer game.

162 GRANDMAMMA'S NEW GAME OF ENGLISH HISTORY, [*after* 1837]. Begins with William the Conqueror and ends with Victoria. An early example of the " Happy Family " card game adapted to history.

163 PETER PARLEY'S ROYAL VICTORIA GAME OF THE KINGS AND QUEENS OF ENGLAND. *Darton and Clark*, [*ca.* 1840]. This, of course, is No. 149 turned into a game. This " Peter Parley"—called "the sixth" by Darton—was Samuel Clark, partner and brother-in-law of J. M. Darton, whose names appear in the imprint.

164 WALLIS'S NEW GAME OF UNIVERSAL HISTORY AND CHRONOLOGY. [*E. Wallis, after* 1840]. This is almost certainly an adaptation of a similar game of earlier date. One of the latest events depicted in this edition is the wedding of Victoria and Albert.

165 A CHAIN OF EVENTS IN ENGLISH HISTORY. *John Betts*, [*after* 1840]. The pictorial case depicts Victoria and Albert.

166 SPOONER'S GAME OF ANCIENT HISTORY. *William Spooner, November 4th*, 1850.

167 SIEGE OF SEBASTOPOL. *Dean & Son*, [*after* 1855].

168 THE SIEGE OF DELHI. *Dean & Son*, [*after* 1857].

169 KINGS AND QUEENS OF FRANCE. [*after* 1851].

170 KINGS AND QUEENS OF ENGLAND. [*ca.* 1860].

171 THE SEVENTEENTH CENTURY. *Jaques* [*ca.* 1880]. Two different versions of this game, both issued by the same publisher.

172 THE EIGHTEENTH CENTURY. *Jaques*, [*ca.* 1880].

173 THE XIXTH CENTURY. *Jaques*, [*ca.* 1890].

(d) Geography.

This subject lends itself, even more than history, to the invention of games popular with children, perhaps because adventure in space is more easily grasped than adventure in time. The enormous popularity of the Robinsonades (see pp. 119 onwards) and the obstinate immortality of Gulliver is eloquent testimony to the fact, and even though such authors as Kingsley and Henty might be quoted to the contrary, it remains true that adventure and exploration are the greater favourites. Even with Amyas Leigh and the various historical heroes of Henty's long series of successes it is hard to decide how much of their romance is derived from their historical background and how much from their wanderings in strange lands.

For this reason we have included lives of Captain Cook, some famous British admirals, and Christopher Columbus in this rather than in the historical section, which surely has only a minor claim to include them. Their adventures would be at least equally thrilling without the adventitious aid of such historical importance as may be their due ; whereas emphasis on that historical importance robs them of most of their charm for the young reader.

Although the " board " games in the geographical line were rather slow off the mark, consisting of little more than an ordinary map fudged up to give it the appearance of a rather unsatisfactory game, there was a reason for this in that the notion of turning geography into a game originated

39

with a map-maker (see p. 186). However, lee-way was quickly made up and these games became more pictorial in character and are among the most successful of the early " board " games.

174 BRIEF DESCRIPTION OF ENGLAND AND WALES (A) . . . VERY PROPER FOR SCHOOLS, TO GIVE YOUTH AN IDEA OF GEOGRAPHY. First edition, 12mo. *Turpin*, [*ca.* 1780]. An extremely interesting volume in which the 52 maps are an old set of geographical playing cards stuck in to serve as illustrations. The cards are fully described and illustrated in Hargrave, *History of Playing Cards*, Boston, 1930, pp. 175-7, which says that they were the first English geographical playing-cards. The complete set is used in the present volume. The four suits are the four parts of England, the 13 northern counties are clubs, the western are spades, the eastern are hearts, and the southern are diamonds. The king of each suit shows a portrait of Charles II and the queen that of Catherine of Braganza. The series was issued in 1675 and the present cards are from the original plates, shewing little signs of wear.

175 THE TRAVELS AND ADVENTURES OF TIMOTHY WILDMAN IN EUROPE, ASIA, AFRICA AND AMERICA. First edition, 12mo. *Luffman, etc.*, [*ca.* 1790].

176 B[ASSAM] (R.). THE FIRST VOYAGE OF COLUMBUS, WHEREIN HE DISCOVERED AMERICA. (2) THE SECOND VOYAGE OF COLUMBUS TO AMERICA. First edition, 2 vols. 12mo. *Bassam, ca.* 1790.

177 A TOUR THROUGH ENGLAND . . . 12mo. *Tabart*, 1806. With a folding engraved map, and six full-page engravings.

178 A TRIP TO PARIS, OF JOHN BULL MOST IN HIS ELEMENT BY HIS FIRESIDE. First edition, sm. 8vo. *Wallis*, [*ca.* 1810]. With 14 coloured cuts.

179 THIRTY-TWO REMARKABLE PLACES IN OLD ENGLAND. FOR THE INSTRUCTION AND ENTERTAINMENT OF YOUTH. First edition, 12mo. *Darton*, [*ca.* 1818]. With 9 full-page engravings of principal towns.

180 TAYLOR (REV. I.). SCENES IN EUROPE, FOR THE AMUSEMENT AND INSTRUCTION OF LITTLE TARRY-AT-HOME TRAVELLERS. First edition, sm. 8vo. *Harris*, 1818. With coloured engraved map and 84 small coloured engravings.

181 ELEMENTS OF GEOGRAPHY (THE). First edition, 8vo. *Newman*, [*ca.* 1820]. With a frontispiece and 12 half-page cuts, all in colour, illustrating geographical features.

182 COOK (CAPTAIN JAMES). THE LIFE OF. 12mo. *Dublin : Jones*, 1824. With numerous cuts.

183 PARK (MUNGO). TRAVELS IN THE INTERIOR OF AFRICA. Sm. 8vo. *Dublin : Hayes*, 1825. With numerous cuts.

184 BEGINNINGS OF GEOGRAPHY. 8vo. *Dean & Co.*, [*ca.* 1850]. An ingeniously arranged book. The general key as frontispiece is referred to by numbers throughout the text, with a series of supplementary smaller illustrations.

185 BETTS'S PORTABLE GLOBE. *John Betts*, [*ca.* 1850]. A pretty, but not very durable toy, the theory of which is that by suitable manipulation of the silk cords the toy can be made to assume the appearance of a terrestrial globe. It *is* possible, but not very practical.

GEOGRAPHICAL GAMES :—

186 NEW ONE SHEET MAP OF THE WORLD LAID
DOWN FROM THE LATEST OBSERVATIONS
AND COMPREHENDING THE NEW DISCOVERIES
TO THE PRESENT TIME. *J. Wallis*, [*after*
1779]. The earliest jig-saw puzzle in the
exhibition and one of the earliest of all. It
can be approximately dated from its
notation of the death of Captain Cook at
Hawaii (here called O'wa-hei-hi). (For a
further note on the history of the jig-saw
puzzle see pp. 185-6).

187 WALLIS'S TOUR THROUGH ENGLAND AND
WALES. A NEW GEOGRAPHICAL PASTIME.
J. Wallis, 24*th December*, 1794. Either
there was a delay in publishing this game,
or there is an earlier issue, for, under 105
in the Directions, the landing of the
Stadtholder of Holland at Harwich on
Jan. 22nd, 1795, is mentioned.

188 WALLIS'S COMPLETE VOYAGE ROUND THE
WORLD. A NEW GEOGRAPHICAL PASTIME.
J. Wallis, *June* 20*th*, 1796. A clear
example of a re-issue, the case being dated
Feb. 27, 1802.

189 PUNCHINELLOGRAPHY OF ENGLAND. BY
MR. WAUTHIER, GEOGR. *Didier & Tebbitt*,
1. *Jany.*, 1808.

190 GEOGRAPHICAL RECREATION, OR A VOYAGE
ROUND THE HABITABLE GLOBE. *J. Harris*,
Octr. 1*st*, 1809. Note the family likeness
to Nos. 154 to 156.

191 THE PANORAMA OF LONDON, OR A DAY'S
JOURNEY ROUND THE METROPOLIS. *J.
Harris*, *Nov.* 1*st*, 1809.

192 WALLIS'S ENTERTAINING AND INSTRUCTIVE TOUR THROUGH THE UNITED KINGDOM OF ENGLAND, SCOTLAND, AND IRELAND ; A NEW GEOGRAPHICAL GAME. COMPREHENDING A DESCRIPTION OF ALL THE CITIES, PRINCIPAL TOWNS, RIVERS, ETC., IN THE BRITISH EMPIRE. *Wallis*, 1811.

193 THE PANORAMA OF EUROPE ... *J. & E. Wallis & J. Wallis Junr., Nov. 1st*, 1815.

194 WALKER'S GEOGRAPHICAL PASTIME, OR TOUR THROUGH THE WESTERN HEMISPHERE. *Darton, 9th May*, 1816. There was a companion game to the Eastern Hemisphere.

195 A SURVEY OF LONDON, BY A PARTY OF TARRY-AT-HOME TRAVELLERS, A NEW GAME TO AMUSE AND INSTRUCT A COMPANY OF FRIENDS BY WILLIAM DARTON. 1820.

196 A GEOGRAPHICAL PANORAMA EXHIBITING CHARACTERISTIC REPRESENTATIONS OF THE SCENERY AND INHABITANTS OF VARIOUS REGIONS. *Harvey & Darton, May 20th*, 1822. This extremely elaborate and attractive toy provides material for eight other scenes of different parts of the world.

197 BETTS'S GEOGRAPHICAL PASTIME. EUROPE DELINEATED. *John Betts, [ca. 1830]*.

198 SCENES IN LONDON. *E. Wallis, [ca. 1830]*.

199 WALLIS'S ELEGANT AND INSTRUCTIVE GAME, EXHIBITING THE WONDERS OF NATURE IN EACH QUARTER OF THE WORLD. *E. Wallis, [ca. 1830]*.

200 PICTORIAL GEOGRAPHY : OR THE PRODUCE AND MANUFACTURES OF THE COUNTIES OF ENGLAND AND WALES. *J. Passmore, [ca. 1835]*.

201 A VOYAGE OF DISCOVERY ; OR THE FIVE WAYFARERS. *William Spooner*, 1836. The teetotum is made in the form of a compass.

202 THE GAME OF VICTORIA, THE QUEEN OF THE SEAS ; DESCRIPTIVE OF GREAT BRITAIN AND HER COLONIAL POSSESSIONS. *E. Wallis* [*after* 1837]. The severely educational nature of this question and answer game contrasts sadly with the gaiety of its picture cards.

203 THE TOUR THROUGH EUROPE. [*ca.* 1840]. An early specimen of the invasion of the British toy-market by the Germans. The tri-lingual lid to the box is very typical.

204 THE TRAVELLERS ; OR, A TOUR THROUGH EUROPE. *William Spooner, Decr. 1st,,* 1842.

205 THE TRAVELLERS OF ENGLAND AND WALES. *William Spooner, Novr. 5th.* 1844.

206 A RIDE THROUGH LONDON. *Dartford, Kent: J. A. Reeves,* [*ca.* 1845]. Note the domino-like cards which are drawn for moves.

207 THE OVERLAND MAIL FROM ENGLAND TO INDIA. *Dartford, Kent : J. A. Reeves,* [*ca.* 1845].

208 THE PIRATE AND THE TRADERS OF THE WEST INDIES. *William Spooner, Nov. 1st,* 1847.

209 BETTS'S TOUR THROUGH EUROPE. *John Betts,* [*ca.* 1845].

210 A TOUR THROUGH THE BRITISH COLONIES. *John Betts,* [*ca.* 1850].

211 THE EARTH AND ITS INHABITANTS. [*ca.* 1850].

212 THE NEW GAME OF THE ASCENT OF MONT BLANC. *Published at the Egyptian Hall, Piccadilly,* [1852]. This and the next number are two instances of the furore created by Albert Smith's illustrated lectures at the Egyptian Hall on his ascent of Mont Blanc.

213 MR. ALBERT SMITH'S ASCENT OF MONT BLANC EVERY EVENING AT THE EGYPTIAN HALL, PICCADILLY. [1852]. A highly ingenious adaptation of the peep-show ; the lid of the box containing the peep-hole, represents the interior of the Egyptian Hall. A series of sixteen interchangeable slides illustrate the crucial points of the narrative. One of them is a transparency of a moonlight scene. Albert Smith himself is depicted in the rostrum.

213a GEOGRAPHICAL AND ZOOLOGICAL GAME OF THE WORLD. *William Spooner, August 14th,* 1852.

214 THE TRAVELLERS OF EUROPE ; WITH IMPROVEMENTS AND ADDITIONS. *William Spooner, December 1st,* 1852. Evidently a re-issue.

215 A VOYAGE ROUND THE WORLD. *John Betts,* [*ca.* 1855].

216 THE YOUNG TRAVELLER'S NEW TOUR THROUGH THE VARIOUS COUNTRIES OF EUROPE. *Jarrold,* [*March,* 1856].

CARD GAMES :—

217 THE GEOGRAPHY OF ENGLAND AND WALES, ACCURATELY DELINEATED ON 52 CARDS. WITH DIRECTIONS FOR PLAYING AN ENTERTAINING GAME. *J. Wallis, Sept. 26th,* 1799. A primitive forerunner of the long-popular card game of the Counties of England. (Compare with Nos. 218 and 222).

218 MRS. G. DARVALL. GEOGRAPHICAL CARDS. EUROPE. *Romsey Press : Printed (for the Author) by John Gray . . . 1834.* Another question and answer game.

219 & 220 COUNTIES OF ENGLAND. FIRST SERIES. *Jaques,* [*ca.* 1880-1890]. Two sets of these cards are shown. The difference in date may be seen from the varying figures given for the population. The later cards do not invariably show an increased population.

221 & 222 COUNTIES OF ENGLAND. 2ND SERIES. *Jaques,* [*ca.* 1880-1890]. Similar differences are observable to those in the first series.

223 THE LIONS OF LONDON. *Ogilvy,* [*ca.* 1890].

THREE RAILWAY GAMES :—

224 WALLIS'S LOCOMOTIVE GAME OF RAIL-ROAD ADVENTURES. *E. Wallis,* [*ca.* 1840].

225 AN ECCENTRIC EXCURSION TO THE CHINESE EMPIRE. *William Spooner, Decr. 1st,* 1843. The four players travel by different routes marked S (for Steam-Boat), W (for Walker), A (for the Aerial or Flying Machine), and R (for Railway). Note the depiction of Henson's " Ariel," for a note on which see No. 981.

226 THE NEW RAILWAY GAME OF THE TOUR THROUGH ENGLAND AND WALES. *J. Passmore* [*ca.* 1850]. A rather catchpenny attempt to sell as a railway game what was little more than a map of England and Wales. The attractive cover has certainly had Wallis's name added, probably because they were especially large scale dealers in such things.

(e) **Languages.**

227 ROBINSON (H.). SCHOLAE WINTONIENSIS PHRASES LATINAE. THE LATINE PHRASES OF WINCHESTER SCHOOL ... *Printed for A. M. and are to be sold by R. Boulter ...* 1670. Note the reference to " Lillie " on the title-page, and compare No. 229. The book is dedicated to the headmaster of Westminster, St. Paul's and Merchant Taylors' Schools, and was very widely used in its time.

228 [COLES (ELISHA)]. NOLENS VOLENS ; OR, YOU SHALL MAKE LATIN WHETHER YOU WILL OR NO, CONTAINING THE PLAINEST DIRECTIONS THAT HAVE YET BEEN GIVEN ON THAT SUBJECT. TOGETHER WITH THE YOUTHS VISIBLE BIBLE : BEING AN ALPHA-BETICAL COLLECTION (FROM THE WHOLE BIBLE) OF SUCH GENERAL HEADS AS WERE JUDG'D MOST CAPABLE OF HIEROGLYPHICS. ILLUSTRATED (WITH GREAT VARIETY) IN FOUR AND TWENTY COPPER PLATES : WITH THE RUDE TRANSLATION OPPOSITE, FOR THE EXERCISE OF THOSE THAT BEGIN TO MAKE LATIN ... First edition, 8vo. *Printed by Andrew Clark for T. Basset, etc.,* 1675. An adaptation of the *Orbis Pictus* of Commenius. An exceedingly rare Latin Grammar not recorded by any of the leading authorities on the subject. Compare No. 231.

229 LILY'S RULES CONSTRUED : WHERE UNTO ARE ADDED THO. ROBINSON'S HETERODITES, THE LATIN SYNTAXIS ... *Buckley and Long-man,* 1736. When Dean Colet founded St. Paul's School in about 1509, he appointed as its first high-master, William Lily or

Lyly, who contributed to Colet's *Aeditia* the Latin Syntax. In one form or another this work was associated with the teaching of Latin in English schools for some three hundred and fifty years. The edition shewn is a late one. It is one of the earliest publishing ventures with which Thomas Longman, founder of the publishing house of Longman, was associated.

230 GREENWOOD (J.). THE LONDON VOCABULARY. ENGLISH AND LATIN : PUT INTO A NEW METHOD . . . Thirteenth edition. *Hitch*, 1759. Originally published in 1711, as *Essay towards a Practical English Grammar*, this work, also by a master of St. Paul's School, had a long and successful career in the present abridged form.

231 — THE SAME. Twenty-first edition. 1797.

232 COMENIUS (J. A.). ORBIS SENSUALIUM PICTUS . . . JOH. AMOS COMENIUS'S VISIBLE WORLD : OR, A NOMENCLATURE OF ALL THE CHIEF THINGS THAT ARE IN THE WORLD, AND OF MEN'S EMPLOYMENT THEREIN ; IN ABOUT 150 CUTS . . . TRANSLATED INTO ENGLISH BY CHARLES HOOLE . . . Twelfth edition, 8vo. *Leacroft*, 1777. This curious work, originally written in " Latin and High-Dutch " and published at Nuremberg in 1657, was the first book, apart from alphabets and catechisms, to be written expressly for children. It is a picture-book and an encyclopedia and had an enormous influence on subsequent books for children. Hundreds of books on his plan were published and as late as 1845 the title " Orbis Pictus " was used for a book of this type. Charles Hoole first translated Comenius into English in 1658, by which time the interest in the book was already on the wane, but the present edition gave it a new vogue.

232a LANCASTER (JOSEPH). THE LINGUIST, OR LITERARY AMUSEMENT. (PART I.). ENGLISH AND FRENCH. *Printed for Joseph Lancaster, by the Lads educated at his Free School, Borough Road ; and sold by Darton and Harvey : and by all the Booksellers in Town and Country, ca.* 1805. The dissenting academies of the eighteenth century were the pioneers of " modern studies," for they taught not only languages but history and geography. Despite the fact that Defoe learned French at Morton's Academy and that Locke in *Of Education,* 1693, spoke of the teaching of French as generally accepted, the practice remained uncommon until the nineteenth century. Adamson (*A Short History of Education,* 1922, 274-5) gives 1836 for its introduction at Shrewsbury, and about the same date for Rugby and Harrow. The elaborate system introduced by Lancaster at this comparatively early date, therefore, is one more tribute to ⋅his pioneering zeal. This appears to be the first time that his teaching of French has been noticed.

233 FENWICK (MRS.). LEÇONS POUR LES ENFANS ... TRADUIT DE L'ANGLOIS PAR L'ABBÉ LE FEBURE. First edition, 12mo. *Godwin,* 1820. With numerous woodcuts.

234 SYLLABAIRE ANGLAIS & FRANÇAIS OU MÉTHODE FACILE POUR ENSEIGNER AUX JEUNES ENFANTS A EPELER ET A LIRE L'ANGLAIS ... PAR BROWN ET J. STEPHENS. 12mo. *Paris :*

Truchy, 1847. With several alphabets on pink paper, and 90 small coloured engravings.

235 MADAME DE CHATELAIN. THE CHILD'S PICTORIAL VOCABULARY FOR TEACHING FAMILIAR PHRASES IN THREE LANGUAGES BY THE AID OF COLOURED ILLUSTRATIONS. First edition, 8vo. *Joseph, Myers & Co.*, 1861. Myers & Co. were largely publishers of English editions of German books and toys for children. They were London agents for the first edition in English of *Struwwelpeter*. The present charmingly illustrated book may have been a French production.

236 MRS PACKER. FRENCH RHYMES FOR THE NURSERY, CONTAINING MORE THAN TWO HUNDRED FAMILIAR NOUNS. *David Nutt*, 1877.

(*f*) Music.

237 A MUSICAL GAME FOR CHILDREN. INVENTED BY L. M. DRUMMOND ESQR. *Didier & Tibbett*, 1806.

238 C. FINCH. THE GAMUT AND TIME-TABLE, IN VERSE. FOR THE INSTRUCTION OF CHILDREN. First edition, sm. 8vo. *Dean and Munday*, [*ca*. 1825]. With frontispiece and 11 woodcuts, all coloured. A charming and ingenious music tutor.

239 THE NURSERY CONCERT; OR MUSICAL EXERCISES OF DUTY AND AFFECTION FOR CHILDREN ... SET TO MUSIC BY S. BENNET, ORGANIST. First edition, sq. 12mo. *Tabart* 1808. With engraved frontispiece of a girl playing a spinet and four large double-pages of engraved music.

240 THE GAME OF THE GAMUT ; A MUSICAL GIFT FOR THE YOUNG. *John Betts*, [*ca.* 1830]. This has no connection, beyond the title, with No. 238.

241 THE FIRST MUSIC BOOK ; OR, GAMUT AND TIME TABLE IN VERSE. *Dean & Son*, [*ca.* 1850]. A later version of No. 238.

242 ROBERT COCKS & CO.'S MUSICAL CARDS. BEING AN EASY METHOD OF LEARNING THE NOTES AND READING AT SIGHT. *Cocks*, [*ca.* 1880].

(g) Astronomy.

243 SCIENCE IN SPORT, OR THE PLEASURES OF ASTRONOMY ... *E. Wallis*, [1810 ?]. This and the next item constitute a minor puzzle. The two are similar and the instruction books both have the imprint of John Wallis and are dated in successive years. This example, however, has on the game itself the imprint of E. Wallis, which is later than either of them. Note that the two games are entirely different in detail, although similar in principle and with identical rules.

244 SCIENCE IN SPORT OR THE PLEASURES OF NATURAL PHILOSOPHY ... *John Wallis*, 1806. An interesting example of a jigsaw puzzle that forms a board game when completed. (See the note to No. 243).

245 PAPA'S TALES ABOUT THE EARTH AND MOON. *A. Park*, [*ca.* 1845].

246 PAPA'S TALES ABOUT THE SUN AND STARS. *A. Park*, [*ca.* 1845].

247 DIAGRAMS ILLUSTRATING THE SCIENCES OF ASTRONOMY AND GEOGRAPHY. *R. Ackermann, etc.*, 1849. Many of the cards are pierced and backed with coloured tissue so that on holding them up to the light it shines through giving the illusion of the sky at night.

(*h*) Law.

248 THE INFANT LAWYER ; OR THE GOVERNMENT OF ENGLAND. EXPLAINED TO THE CAPACITY OF YOUTH. THIS IS A PROPER NEW YEAR'S GIFT FROM A FATHER. First edition, 12mo. *Marshall*, [*ca.* 1785]. Engraved frontispiece of the Commons in session.

249 TAYLOR (J.). PARLOUR COMMENTARIES ON THE CONSTITUTION AND LAWS OF ENGLAND. First edition, 8vo. *Harris*, 1825. With engraved title and six half-page engravings all in colour.

(*i*) Deportment, Manners, etc.

This section demands a short note on two remarkable features of the books in it. First, the revolting priggishness observable in the tone and tenor of most of the books, which comes out in the titles (*e.g.*, No. 252 " Mary Sensible," " Eliza Thoughtful," etc.) and in the sentiments of the writers (see especially the captions to No. 254). The other point is the general tendency to treat children as miniature adults ; no other justification can be found for the elaborate instruction in carving given in No. 251.

250 A MUSEUM FOR YOUNG GENTLEMEN AND LADIES ; OR, A PRIVATE TUTOR FOR LITTLE MASTERS AND MISSES ... First edition, sq. 12mo. *Printed for J. Hodges, on the Bridge ; J. Newbery, in St. Paul's Church Yard ; and B. Collins, in Salisbury.* [1750]. Extremely rare. Gumuchian who, without evidence, attributes it to Goldsmith, catalogues the edition of 1784, published by Carnan-Welsh, pp. 273-5, quotes it from Newbery's list of 1758, describes the 8th edition of 1776 from the copy in the South Kensington Museum, but transcribes the advertisement of the first edition from the *General Evening Post* of July 26, 1750. Profusely illustrated with small cuts.

251 [THE REV. JOHN TRUSLER]. THE HONOURS OF THE TABLE, OR, RULES FOR BEHAVIOUR DURING MEALS ... FOR THE USE OF YOUNG PEOPLE. Sm. 8vo. *Literary Press,* 1791. With numerous cuts in the text.

252 TEA-TABLE DIALOGUES, BETWEEN A GOVERNESS AND MARY SENSIBLE, ELIZA THOUGHTFUL [AND FIVE OTHERS]. First edition, 16mo. *Darton,* 1803. With 12 small woodcuts.

253 ARABELLA ANGUS. THE JUVENILE SPECTATOR ; BEING OBSERVATIONS ON THE TEMPERS, MANNERS, AND FOIBLES OF VARIOUS YOUNG PERSONS. First edition, 8vo., *Darton,* 1810. With 4 copper engravings.

254 THE GOOD BOY'S SOLILOQUY ; CONTAINING HIS PARENTS' INSTRUCTIONS RELATIVE TO HIS DISPOSITION AND MANNERS. BY THE AUTHOR OF " THE INVITED ALPHABET,"

ETC. First edition, sq. 12mo. *Darton,* 1811. With 16 full-page engravings each illustrating something the Good Boy must do.

255 JUVENILE INCIDENTS OR THE STUDIES AND AMUSEMENTS OF A DAY. First edition, 12mo. *Edinburgh* : *Oliver and Boyd, ca.* 1820.

(*j*) Natural History.

A colourful subject in which the interest of children is easily and eternally aroused. The early books were written by hacks or amateurs and the level of accuracy is not very high—a contrast to the modern practice where experts are engaged for such collections as the "Wayside and Woodland," the "Observer," and the "King Penguin" Series. The older books, however, at least hold their own in the attraction of their illustrations. (*Cf.* Nos. 554 to 585).

256 WARD (THE REV. SAMUEL). A MODERN SYSTEM OF NATURAL HISTORY, CONTAINING ACCURATE DESCRIPTIONS, AND FAITHFUL HISTORIES OF ANIMALS, VEGETABLES, AND MINERALS . . . First edition, 12 vols. *F. Newbery,* 1775-6. Welsh calls this " a very ambitious work." Profusely illustrated with copper plates.

257 JUVENILE RAMBLES THROUGH THE PATHS OF NATURE ; IN WHICH MANY PARTS OF THE WONDERFUL WORKS OF CREATION ARE BROUGHT FORWARD. First edition, 16mo. *E. Newbery,* [*ca.* 1786]. Numerous wood-cuts in the text, all coloured by hand.

258 THE NATURAL HISTORY OF BIRDS ... ILLUSTRATED BY A GREAT VARIETY OF COPPER PLATES, COMPRISING NEAR ONE HUNDRED FIGURES. *Newbery*, 1793. Welsh records this edition, but does not describe it. It may be a new edition of one part of Brooke's "Natural History," and if this is so, the introduction is by Goldsmith.

259 VIETH (G. U. A.). THE PLEASING PRECEPTOR : OR FAMILIAR INSTRUCTIONS IN NATURAL HISTORY AND PHYSICS, ADAPTED TO THE CAPACITIES OF YOUTH ... First edition, 2 vols., sm. 8vo. *Robinson*, 1800. With folding coloured frontispiece and cuts in the text.

260 MARSHALL'S HISTORY OF BIRDS. First edition, 12mo. *Marshall*, [1803]. With 26 full-page coloured engravings of birds.

261 FOOTSTEPS TO THE NATURAL HISTORY OF BEASTS AND BIRDS. PART I. First edition, 12mo. *Darton*, 1804.

262 W. BELCH'S HISTORY OF FISHES AND INSECTS. *Belch*, [ca. 1815].

263 TOMMY TRIP'S MUSEUM ; OR A PEEP AT THE QUADRUPED RACE. *J. Harris and Son*, [ca. 1820]. Evidence of the continued interest in an old favourite. Tommy Trip was one of the original Newbery's earliest and most felicitous inventions.

263a MYRIANTHEA ; OR, NUMBERLESS GROUPS OF CHANGEABLE FLOWERS : INTENDED TO TEACH, BY THE MOST READY AND EASY MEANS, THE ART OF COMPOSING, DRAWING AND COLOURED GROUPS OF FLOWERS .. *J. Burgis, etc., ca.* 1820.

264 A REPRESENTATION OF THIRTY-SIX BIRDS COMMONLY SEEN IN ENGLAND. *J. Marshall May 8th*, 1821. A charming jig-saw puzzle in which colour is used in a similar style to the illustrated books of the period.

265 THE AVIARY ; OR, AGREABLE VISIT. INTENDED FOR CHILDREN. First edition, 12mo. *Darton*, 1824.

266 FAIRBURN'S PEEP INTO NATURAL HISTORY. First edition, 12mo. *Fairburn*, [*ca*. 1825]. With coloured title, large folding coloured frontispiece and 19 coloured woodcuts of birds and animals.

267 [BEWICK (T.)]. THE YOUNGSTER'S DIARY ; OR YOUTH'S REMEMBRANCER OF NATURAL EVENTS FOR EVERY MONTH IN THE YEAR. First edition, 12mo. *Alnwick* : *Davison*, N.D. Hugo (309), 285. With 35 Bewick cuts.

268 [BEWICK (T.)]. A NATURAL HISTORY OF (1) BRITISH BIRDS, (2) BRITISH QUADRUPEDS, (3) WATER BIRDS, (4) FISHES, (5) REPTILES, SERPENTS AND INSECTS, (6) FOREIGN BIRDS, (7) FOREIGN QUADRUPEDS. First editions, 7 vols., 12mo. *Alnwick* : *Davison*, [*ca*. 1808]. With, in all, 236 woodcuts by Bewick.

269 FANNY AND MARY ; OR, JUVENILE VIEWS OF HAPPINESS. First edition, sq. 12mo. *Harvey and Darton*, 1821. With four engravings, the frontispiece showing " The Curious Animal from New Holland " (*i.e.*, a duck-billed platypus).

270 MRS. RITSON. SPRING FLOWERS ; OR, EARLY LESSONS FOR YOUNG CHILDREN, NOT EXCEEDING WORDS OF TWO SYLLABLES . . . *Harris*, 1825. With 15 small coloured woodcuts.

271 WONDERS ! DESCRIPTIVE OF SOME OF THE MOST REMARKABLE OF NATURE AND ART. First edition, sm. 8vo. *Harris*, 1823. With 16 half-page woodcuts in colour.

272 THE WONDERS OF ART IN ALL THE QUARTERS OF THE WORLD. *E. Wallis*, [*ca.* 1823]. This game bears a strong family likeness to the preceding number. The balloon and parachute shewn are of the Garnerin type.

273 BIRD-CATCHING ; OR, THE NORTHERN ADVENTURES. BEING AN ACCOUNT OF SEVERAL METHODS OF TAKING BIRDS IN THE FAROE ISLANDS ... INTENDED FOR CHILDREN. First edition, fcap. 8vo. *Darton*, 1823. With 8 half-page engravings.

274 WILSON (REV. T.). THE LITTLE MINERALOGIST. (2) THE LITTLE CONCHOLOGIST. (3) THE LITTLE GEOLOGIST. (4) THE LITTLE MARINE BOTANIST. *Darton and Clark*, [*ca.* 1840]. Four works bound in one volume. The last is printed on pink paper.

275 HART (MARY KERR). THE MOSS ROSE'S CONVERSAZIONE : A NOVELTY FOR THE SEASON. *W. & H. Rock*, [*ca.* 1840]. The coloured borders to the cards are very typical of the period.

276 GRAPHIC ILLUSTRATIONS OF ANIMALS, SHOWING THEIR UTILITY TO MAN ... *Roake and Varty*, [*ca.* 1843]. In the four original parts. A coloured copy.

277 INSECTS. ENTOMOLOGY. *Darton and Clark*, [*ca.* 1845]. One of a series of coloured sheets on natural history subjects.

278 ANIMALS FROM NOAH'S ARK, WITH SOME ATTENTION TO THEIR COMPARATIVE SIZES. *Thomas Dean and Son*, [*ca.* 1850]. This is an inferior version of an earlier publication. The animals include some quite unfamiliar to Noah. *e.g.*, Newfoundland, Mastiff, Shetland Pony, Kangaroo, and, most ludicrous of all, a Spaniel, " quite the Lady's dog," in very Victorian surroundings. At least 12 sheets were issued.

279 GARDEN FLOWERS. A NEW CARD GAME. [*ca.* 1860]. A matching game in which the correct names had to be fitted to the picture cards.

PART II

Nursery Rhymes and other Verses

We begin here with some of the famous Dames of the Nursery, the first of them the most famous of all—" Old Mother Hubbard." It is curious to observe that, although the rhyme has retained its attraction for children to this day, the name of the author has been almost completely forgotten, and is hardly ever used on the title-pages of modern editions of the book. Very little is known about her beyond the scanty information given on the slip-case of No. 281. Her " Continuation " of the rhyme seems to have fallen flat and is not used in modern versions.

The success of the book was immediate and considerable, however, and it had many imitators, some of which are shewn here.

With the next rhyme—*The House that Jack Built*—we had to content ourselves with a rather meagre shewing. We can say nothing certain as to the origin or antiquity of it except that it considerably ante-dates anything included here. Indeed one of the imitations (No. 302) is about twenty years earlier than any edition of the original in the exhibition. The rhyme was already familiar in the late eighteenth century, evidence of which may be derived from the enormous success which attended William Hone's parody of it attacking the Prince Regent—*The Political House that Jack Built*—which was itself the subject of numerous imitations.

Cock Robin probably made his first appearance in the nursery in the second half of the eighteenth century in substantially the form in which we know him to-day. The earliest version here is a chapbook of 1800 which varies very little from the modern text. Harris appears to have been the first to see the possibility of making the original rhyme a sequel by providing an account of Cock Robin's marriage to Jenny Wren which should end with the death of the groom (see No. 307). The narrative bears a striking resemblance in style and construction to *The Butterfly's Ball*, first published in 1807, but there appears to be no ground for the suggestion that Roscoe may have been influenced by it. The biological improbability of the title may have had something to do with its short-lived popularity. A fair sprinkling of other nursery favourites is followed by some collections of nursery rhymes, and by other verse for children.

Finally, in this section, comes *The Butterfly's Ball* and a few of its sequels. Normally, once a book has firmly established a claim to the affections of children, its popularity persists in subsequent generations. *The Butterfly's Ball* is, perhaps, the most notable exception. In its day it was the most widely successful, and frequently reprinted and imitated of all children's books of its day, but it is now almost forgotten.

William Roscoe, its author, was a historian living in Liverpool, the author of such serious (and almost equally forgotten) works as the lives of Lorenzo de Medici and Pope Leo X, and a botanist of some note, responsible, among other things, for a monograph on *Monandrian Plants of the Order Scitameneae.* He wrote *The Butterfly's Ball* to amuse his own children, but after its publication in the *Gentleman's Magazine* in November, 1806, it attracted the attention of John Harris, who issued it in slightly abbreviated form in 1807. George III had it set to music by Sir George Smart for the young princesses and Harris proceeded to sell at least 20,000 copies of the publication inside twelve months.

Harris commissioned Catharine Anne Dorset, a decayed gentlewoman, to provide a sequel called *The Peacock at Home*, which was almost equally successful, and the spate of sequels and imitations began. There were many others besides those shewn here.

280 [SARAH CATHERINE MARTIN]. THE COMIC ADVENTURES OF OLD MOTHER HUBBARD AND HER DOG. CONTINUATION OF THE COMIC ADVENTURES OF OLD MOTHER HUBBARD ... *Harris*, 1805-1806. Three volumes, comprising the first and second editions of the first part and the first edition of the second part.

281 SARAH CATHERINE MARTIN. FACSIMILE OF THE ORIGINAL MANUSCRIPT OF OLD MOTHER HUBBARD. *Oxford University Press*, N.D. The label on the slip-case tells the story of this world-famous nursery rhyme in brief.

282 OLD MOTHER HUBBARD AND HER DOG. *D. Carvalho, ca.* 1820. One of a series of nursery rhymes, including *A, Apple Pie, Tommy Tucker, Little Jack Horner,* etc., originally published separately but here collected and called *The Nursery Present.*

283 MOTHER HUBBARD, AND HER DOG ... *Derby* : *Thomas Richardson, ca.* 1825. An early chapbook version, price threepence.

284 OLD MOTHER HUBBARD AND HER DOG. *London and Otley* : *Wm. Walker and Son, ca.* 1840. In Walker's " Illuminated Library."

285 OLD MOTHER HUBBARD OF 1793 ... OLD MOTHER HUBBARD OF TO-DAY. *Dean & Son*, [1893]. A gross piece of falsification. The dates in the facsimile of the original edition have been altered to make it appear that this edition is the centenary one. No. 281 clearly shows that the rhyme was not written until 1804.

286 A TRUE HISTORY OF A LITTLE OLD WOMAN WHO FOUND A SILVER PENNY. First edition, sq. 12mo. *Tabart*, 1806. This appears to be the original version of the nursery classic of the old woman's efforts to induce her pig to get over a stile. With 14 full-page hand-coloured engravings.

287 THE OLD WOMAN AND HER SILVER PENNY. ILLUSTRATED BY CRUIKSHANK. *Read & Co., ca.* 1860. A prose version. The illustrator is Percy Cruikshank.

288 OLD WOMAN AND HER SILVER PENNY. *Dean & Son, ca.* 1865. One of Dean's Moveable Books. This version begins to approximate to the modern one.

289 CONTINUATION OF THE ADVENTURES OF DAME TROT, AND HER COMICAL CAT. 1806. There is no early edition of the first part of Dame Trot in the collection, but we are able to show three varieties of the second part. The first is published by Harris, the second is Darton's, and the third has no publisher's name, all published in 1806.

290 OLD DAME TROT AND HER CAT. *London and Otley : Wm. Walker and Son, ca.* 1840. In Walker's " Illuminated Library."

290a KOMISCHE ABENTHEUER MADAME TROTT MIT IHRER KATZE. *Mainz : J. Schultz.* A rare German translation of Dame Trot, with all the original adventures.

291 THE ACCOUNT OF THE OLD WOMAN WHO SOLD FRUIT ; SHEWING HOW SHE GOT TIPSEY, HER FRUIT STOLEN, AND HER REFORMATION. First edition, 12mo. *Lane, 1st Jan.,* 1807.

292 THE TRAGICAL WANDERINGS AND ADVENTURES OF GRIMALKIN, THE ELDEST SON OF DAME TROT'S CAT. First edition, sq. 12mo. *Tabart,* 1808. Extremely rare. With 10 charming full-page coloured engravings.

293 DAME PARTLET'S FARM ; AN ACCOUNT OF THE RICHES SHE OBTAINED BY INDUSTRY, THE GOOD LIFE SHE LED, AND ALAS ! GOOD READER, HER DEATH AND EPITAPH. First edition, fcap. 8vo. *Harris*, [1834]. With 12 charming half-page engravings in colour.

294 THE OLD WOMAN AND HER THREE SONS. First edition, sq. 12mo. *Harris*, 1815.

295 DAME WIGGINS OF LEE, AND HER SEVEN WONDERFUL CATS. A HUMOROUS TALE. WRITTEN PRINCIPALLY BY A LADY OF NINETY. First edition, sm. 8vo. *Newman*, 1823. Extremely rare. A coloured copy. The book was also published simultaneously by Dean and Munday.

296 DAME WIGGINS OF LEE ... *Thos. Dean & Co.*, *ca.* 1840.

297 DAME DUMPLING'S TRIP TO MARKET. Second edition, sm. 8vo. *E. Wallis*, [*ca.* 1825].

298 LITTLE DAME CRUMP. *Dean & Son*, *ca.* 1865. A new (and inferior) version of the *Old Woman and Her Silver Penny*.

299 THE HISTORY OF THE HOUSE THAT JACK BUILT. *D. Carvalho*, *ca.* 1820.

300 THE HOUSE THAT JACK BUILT, TOGETHER WITH HIS ALPHABET AND LESSONS. 12mo. *Darton*, [*ca.* 1820].

301 THE HOUSE THAT JACK BUILT. *Alnwick* : *Davison*, [*ca.* 1825]. A halfpenny chapbook with Bewick cuts.

301a THE HOUSE THAT JACK BUILT. *Routledge*, *ca.* 1880. The first edition of the version illustrated by Caldecott.

302 BISSET (J.). JUVENILE REDUPLICATIONS : OR, THE NEW " HOUSE THAT JACK BUILT " ... First edition, sm. 8vo. *Birmingham*: *Grafton & Reddell, etc.*, 1800. With engraved frontispiece by the author, of himself with his book, and 12 woodcut head-pieces.

303 THE NEW HOUSE THAT JACK BUILT. Sm. 8vo. *Hodgson*, 1822. This is quite different from No. 302 and is, indeed, little more than the original rhyme pepped up with a strong moral flavour.

304 THE OAK AT BOSCOBEL ; A NEW AND INGENIOUS PARODY ON THE HOUSE THAT JACK BUILT. First edition, sq. 12mo. *Harris*, 1813. 12 hand-coloured engravings.

305 FEMALE TRIUMPH ! OR THE DEFEAT OF THE ORANGE. First edition, sq. 12mo. *Blackman*, 1816. The form of this is clearly derived from *The House that Jack Built*.

306 AN ELEGY ON THE DEATH AND BURIAL OF COCK ROBIN, ALSO THE PLEASING STORY OF THE HOUSE THAT JACK BUILT. 24mo. *Gainsborough* : *Mozley*, 1800. A charming chapbook, with frontispiece and 26 small woodcuts in the Bewick style.

307 THE COURTSHIP, MARRIAGE AND PIC-NIC DINNER, OF COCK ROBIN, AND JENNY WREN. TO WHICH IS ADDED, ALAS ! THE DOLEFUL DEATH OF THE BRIDEGROOM. *Harris*, 1806.

308 COCK ROBIN AND JENNY WREN ... *Harris*, 1807. A reprint of No. 307 issued in the following year. Note how the plates have deteriorated. (*Cf.* also Nos. 756a and b).

309 DEATH AND BURIAL OF COCK ROBIN. *Hodgson, ca.* 1820. This volume is a collection of nursery rhymes, each of which was originally issued separately, now bound together and called *Peter Parley's Present.* This title, and the cloth binding suggest a date in the 'thirties for the issue of the volume. The first booklet in the volume is the *Courtship and Marriage of Jenny Wren and Cock Robin,* concluding with the death of the latter.

310 THE DEATH AND BURIAL OF POOR COCK ROBIN. *Dean & Munday,* [*ca.* 1820].

311 COCK ROBIN. *J. March, ca.* 1830.

312 DEATH AND BURIAL OF COCK ROBIN : AND TRIAL OF COCK SPARROW. *W. S. Johnson, ca.* 1840. A new version of the old rhyme, issued in panorama form by a printer of the Catnach Press type.

313 LITTLE COCK ROBIN PICTORIAL QUADRILLES BY CHARLES D'ALBERT. Folio. *Chappell,* [*ca.* 1860]. With coloured vignette on wrapper and five charming circular head-pieces in colour of scenes from the Death of Cock Robin.

314 PUNCH OR A COLLECTION OF DROLL FIGURES PROPER FOR CHILDREN TO DRAW AFTER. *Sayer,* [*ca.* 1780]. Sixteen engravings on 8 leaves, stitched as issued.

315 THE TRAGICAL COMEDY OF PUNCH AND JUDY. *Martin,* [*ca.* 1820]. With vignette title and 12 illustrations all coloured.

316 PUNCH, JUDY, AND DOG TOBY AS CUT-OUT FIGURES. *ca.* 1850.

317 PUNCH AND JUDY. *Frederick Warne, ca.* 1865.

318 HUMPTY DUMPTY. Oblong 8vo. *Tilt & Bogue,* 1843. A curious coloured panorama. Note the translations of the rhyme on the end-paper.

319 HUMPTY DUMPTY. *Gowan & Standing, ca.* 1865.

320 THE QUEEN OF HEARTS. *Routledge, ca.* 1880. The first edition of Caldecott's version. (Cf. No. 712).

321 THE WHOLE PARTICULARS OF SAM AND HIS GUN . . . [*ca.* 1810]. An early version of : "There was a little man And he had a little gun . . ."

322 SIMPLE SIMON. *T. Batchelar, ca.* 1810. With 16 woodcut headpieces with a verse below each.

323 THREE LITTLE KITTENS. BY COMUS. *Nelson,* 1859. This is an elaborate prose version introducing the rhymes at apposite points in the narrative.

324 HISTORY OF THE THREE LITTLE KITTENS WHO LOST THEIR MITTENS. *Dean & Son, ca.* 1865. A Moveable Book.

325 TOM, THE PIPER'S SON. *March, ca.* 1850.

326 MOTHER GOOSE'S MELODY ; OR, SONNETS FOR THE CRADLE : CONTAINING THE MOST CELEBRATED SONGS AND LULLABIES OF THE OLD BRITISH NURSES. *Marshall,* [1803]. With engraved frontispiece and numerous cuts in the text. An extremely rare edition of a favourite collection. The only other recorded copy of it is in the Bodleian Library. Ours is an extremely interesting copy, a contemporary hand has added extra lines to some of the rhymes and has added other nursery rhymes with suitable vignette drawings, as though for an enlarged edition. The rhymes include : Boys and girls come out to play ; Dickery, dickery, dock ; Bah ! bah ! black sheep ; Little Tom Tucker ; Jack and Gill (*sic*) ; etc.

327 GAMMER GURTON'S GARLAND ; OR, THE NURSERY PARNASSUS ... First edition, 8vo. *Triphook*, 1820. Includes : The Lady and the Swine ; London Bridge is Broken Down ; Ding dong Bell ; Song of Sixpence ; Hey diddle-diddle; etc.

328 TOMMY THUMB'S SONG-BOOK, FOR ALL LITTLE MASTERS AND MISSES ... BY NURSE LOVE-CHILD. First edition, 24mo. *Glasgow* : *Lumsden*, 1815. Includes : Baby Bunting ; Hushaby Baby ; Patty Cake, Patty Cake ; etc. The 29 woodcuts are said by Hugo, No. (323) to be " possibly by Thomas Bewick."

329 GRANDMAMMA'S NURSERY RHYMES ; OR, AMUSEMENTS FOR CHILDREN AT HOME. *J. Fairburn*, *ca.* 1825. Includes : Baa, baa, black sheep ; Ride a cock horse ; Little Jack Horner ; Little Boy Blue ; etc.

330 THE CHILD'S TREASURY OF KNOWLEDGE AND AMUSEMENT ; OR, REUBEN RAMBLE'S PICTURE LESSONS. First edition, 8vo. *Darton and Clark*, *ca.* 1845. Another example of using up old stock, several booklets bound into one, the first of which is *Songs for the Nursery*, which includes : One, two, buckle my shoe ; Little Bo-peep has lost her sheep ; The Lion and the Unicorn ; This little Pig ; etc.

331 NURSERY SONGS. A BOX OF PICTURE BRICKS. *ca.* 1850. There are six sets of pictures in all. In the one shewn six rhymes are illustrated : Little Miss Muffett ; Hey, diddle, diddle ; See-saw, Jack in a hedge ; Simple Simon ; This little Pig ; The Old Woman who lived in a shoe. Each of the other sets illustrates one story only : Sing a Song of Sixpence ; The House that Jack Built ; Cock Robin ; Mother Hubbard ; Punch and Judy. There are picture-sheets with rhymes to each set of bricks.

332 [THOMAS FOXTON]. MORAL SONGS COMPOSED FOR THE USE OF CHILDREN, RECOMMENDED BY THE REVEREND ISAAC WATTS, D.D. . . . *Aaron Ward,* 1743. One knows not whether to admire most the author's modesty in omitting his own name from the title, or his perspicacit y in cashing-in on the eminence of Dr. Watts.

333 TOMMY TAGG. A COLLECTION OF PRETTY POEMS FOR THE AMUSEMENT OF CHILDREN THREE FOOT HIGH. " The Fifty Fourth Edition," 16mo. *Printed for the Booksellers of Europe, Asia, Africa, and America, and sold at the Bible and Sun, in St. Paul's Church-Yard,* 1756. Exceedingly rare. The publisher, of course, was Newbery, and " Fifty Fourth Edition " is clearly a joke on his part. Welsh, p. 294, takes the title from a list of about 1758, but describes only an edition of 1777 which is in the Bodleian Library, but lacks the title-page. There are about 60 excellent woodcuts, of which one on p. 7 depicts a Printer composing the Lilliputian Magazine ; another, on p. 77, A Merry Andrew at Southwark Fair ; and several are of hunting scenes. The poem is of " Inkle and Yarico."

334 THE HUMOURS OF THE FAIR —A TALE FOR THE NURSERY. [*ca.* 1805]. Sq. 12mo.

335 MEMOIRS OF THE LITTLE MAN AND THE LITTLE MAID ::: First edition, sq. 12mo. *Tabart*, 1807. With 12 coloured engravings.

336 COBBLER ! STICK TO YOUR LAST ; OR THE ADVENTURES OF JOE DOBSON. BY B.A.T. First edition, sq. 12mo. *Harris*, 1807. Sixteen full-page coloured engravings, and engraved text.

337 THE DAISY ; OR CAUTIONARY STORIES IN VERSE. ADAPTED TO THE IDEAS OF CHILDREN FROM FOUR TO EIGHT YEARS OLD. First edition, 12mo. *Harris*, 1807. Extremely scarce and very frequently reprinted. With 30 full-page coloured cuts.

338 [O'KEEFFE (A.)]. ORIGINAL POEMS ; CALCULATED TO IMPROVE THE MIND OF YOUTH, AND ALLURE IT TO VIRTUE. BY ADELAIDE. PART I. First edition, sq. 12mo. *Harris*, 1808. With engraved frontispiece and 8 full-page engravings.

339 THE CONJUROR ; OR THE TURKEY AND THE RING. First edition, sq. 12mo. *Dutton*, 1808.

340 SIMPLE STORIES ; IN VERSE. BEING A COLLECTION OF ORIGINAL POEMS ; DESIGNED FOR THE USE OF CHILDREN. First edition, sm. 8vo. *Tabart*, 1809. With 12 charming full-page coloured engravings.

341 CHARLES MORETON. THE MAID AND THE MAGPIE, AN INTERESTING TALE, FOUNDED ON FACTS. First edition, sq. 12mo. *Stevens*, *ca.* 1810. With engraved title and frontispiece, and 6 coloured engravings.

342 VERSES FOR LITTLE CHILDREN. WRITTEN BY A YOUNG LADY FOR THE AMUSEMENT OF HER JUNIOR BROTHERS AND SISTERS. First edition, sq. 12mo. *Darton*, 1813. With 4 full-page engravings.

343 THE KEEPSAKE ; OR, POEMS AND PICTURES FOR CHILDHOOD AND YOUTH. First edition, sm. 8vo. *Darton*, 1818. With 17 charming coloured engravings.

344 THE CROCUS, CONTAINING ORIGINAL POEMS FOR YOUNG PEOPLE. BY J. E. M. First edition, sm. 8vo. *Darton*, [*ca.* 1820]. With 12 half-page engravings in colour.

The " Butterfly's Ball " and its Imitators.

345 ROSCOE (WILLIAM). THE ORIGINAL HOLOGRAPH MANUSCRIPT OF *The Butterfly's Ball*, entirely in his hand. In twelve stanzas of four lines each, written on three sides of a double quarto sheet (watermarked " I. Taylor, 1799 "), and concluding with a poem of three four-line stanzas by him—THE SQUIRREL—also in his hand. The original manuscript of a nursery poem which was once as famous and popular as " Alice in Wonderland." Its vogue was enormous and the selection of imitations of, and sequels to the poem shewn here, gives a slight indication of how popular it was. For a note on the author and his work see the preamble to this section.

Four verses are included in the manuscript which were not printed in the first edition. It appears to have been in the possession of his son Thomas, editor of *The Juvenile Keepsake*, 1828-30, and bears his signature at the head of the first page. The MS. is endorsed in pencil on the back " The Butterfly's Ball from Mr. Roscoe "—presumably in the hand of John Harris who published it in 1807.

347 [MRS. DORSET]. THE PEACOCK " AT HOME " : A SEQUEL TO THE BUTTERFLY'S BALL. WRITTEN BY A LADY. First edition, 12mo. *Harris*, 1807. The six coloured engravings are after Mulready. The first and most consistently popular of the sequels.

347a THE PEACOCK " AT HOME " . . . TO WHICH IS ADDED THE BUTTERFLY'S BALL. Fcap. 8vo. *Harris*, 1822. This edition has an entirely new series of eight coloured woodcuts.

347b THE PEACOCK AT HOME. A MERRY GAME. *Nichols, ca.* 1835. A card game in which all Mrs. Dorset's characters are introduced.

348 [MRS. DORSET (?)]. THE LION'S MASQUERADE. First edition, sq. 12mo. *J. Harris*, 1807.

349 THE BUTTERFLY'S FUNERAL. A SEQUEL TO THE BUTTERFLY'S BALL . . . BY J. L. B. First edition, sq. 12mo. *J. Wallis, Jr.*, 1808.

350 THE COURT OF THE BEASTS. *Printed for the Author, and sold by Darton and Harvey*, 1808. First edition, cr. 8vo. With 4 full-page engravings.

351 THE EAGLE'S MASQUE. BY TOM TIT. First edition, sm. 8vo. *Mawman*, 1808. With 6 full-page engravings.

352 THE FISHES' FEAST, WITH A MERMAID'S SONG, DEDICATED TO THE AUTHOR OF THE " PEACOCK AT HOME " . . . TO WHICH IS ADDED THE APE'S CONCERT. First edition, 8vo. *Spencer*, 1808. With 2 engravings.

353 MRS. COCKLE. THE FISHES GRAND GALA. A COMPANION TO THE " PEACOCK AT HOME," ETC., ETC. First edition, 2 vols., sq. 12mo. Part I has 6 coloured and Part II 5 uncoloured engravings.

354 THE HORSE'S LEVEE, OR THE COURT OF PEGASUS. INTENDED AS A COMPANION TO THE BUTTERFLY'S BALL ... First edition, 12mo. *Harris*, 1803. With frontispiece and 6 full-page engravings.

355 THE JACK DAW " AT HOME " ; BY A YOUNG LADY OF RANK. First edition, sq. 12mo. *Didier and Tebbett*, 1808. With 4 copper-plates.

356 THE LOBSTER'S VOYAGE TO THE BRAZILS. First edition, sq. 12mo. *Harris*, 1808. A coloured copy.

357 THE ROSE'S BREAKFAST ; TRIFLES IN PROSE TO INSTRUCT AND AMUSE THE YOUNG. First edition, sq. 12mo. *Harris*, 1808. A coloured copy.

358 [ANN TAYLOR]. THE WEDDING AMONG THE FLOWERS. BY ONE OF THE AUTHORS OF ... RHYMES FOR THE NURSERY, ETC. *First edition*, sq. 12mo. *Darton*, 1808. With frontispiece and 3 other charming engravings. Darton paid Miss Taylor twelve guineas for the poem, which she thought " a munificent gift."

359 [MRS. DORSET]. THE BUTTERFLY'S BIRTH-DAY. BY THE AUTHOR OF THE BUTTERFLY'S BALL. First edition, sq. 12mo. *Longman*, 1809. With 5 copper engravings.

360 THE MERMAID " AT HOME." First edition, 12mo. *J. Harris*, 1809.

361 MRS. REEVE. THE FLOWERS AT COURT. First edition, sm. 8vo. *Author, etc.*, 1809. With 6 original water-colour drawings of flowers by the author.

362 MRS. B. HOOLE. LA FETE DE LA ROSE ; OR THE DRAMATIC FLOWERS. A HOLIDAY PRESENT, FOR YOUNG PEOPLE. Third edition, sq. 12mo. *Knaresborough : Printed by Hargrove & Sons . . .* 1810.

363 POMONA'S FROLIC : OR, THE GRAND JUBILEE OF THE ANIMATED FRUIT. First edition, 2 vols., sq. 12mo. *Minerva Press*, 1810. Each part has 6 full-page coloured engravings. All the characters are taken by and portrayed as different fruits.

364 THE TURTLE DOVE'S WEDDING. A POEM. First edition, sm. 8vo. *Wallis, [ca.* 1810]. Engraved throughout, with 16 coloured plates.

365 MADAME GRIMALKIN'S PARTY. Third edition, sq. 12mo. *Printed at the Minerva Press, for A. K. Newman & Co.*, 1811.

366 THE DANDIE'S BALL ; OR HIGH LIFE IN THE CITY. First edition, 8vo. *Marshall*, 1819. A very rare book, with frontispiece, vignette title, and 14 half-page plates, all coloured engravings by R. Cruikshank.

367 THE BUTTERFLY'S BALL, ETC. Three of Charles Welsh's facsimile reprints of early editions of these old favourites, with bibliographical forewords. *Published by Griffith & Farran, successors to John Harris, in* 1883.

PART III

Story Books

SECTION I: CHAPBOOKS

Among the earliest purveyors of books for children were peripatetic pedlars, known as chapmen. The use of the word in England is very ancient ; the Oxford Dictionary mentions it in the ninth century, when its meaning was already synonymous with, perhaps even actually in the form " cheapmen." They were bagmen travelling the countryside and penetrating to villages and homesteads remote from shops of any kind. Some idea of the wares they carried may be gathered from an advertisement of John Marshall in 1708. He was prepared to supply them not only with all sorts of books, broadsides and ballads, but with Lottery Pictures, London Cries, labels for cases of household remedies, Venice-Treacle, Funeral Tickets, Receipts for Land-Tax, and Affidavits for Burials in Woollen (a reminder of the sumptuary laws).

Books, however, formed a prominent feature of their stock-in-trade very early on ; in 1592 Chettle, in *Kind-Harts*, has a reference to " Chapmen, able to spred more pamphlets . . . than all the booksellers in London."

The imprints on these crudely produced booklets refer to the chapmen as " Walking," " Running," " Travelling," and even " Flying " Stationers, further evidence of their importance as purveyors of reading matter.

Their stocks were not, of course, confined to books for children, and most of the early juvenile literature they carried was confined to deeds of "derring do," recounting the exploits of such heroes as Guy of Warwick, Robin Hood, and the Seven Champions of Christendom. Seventeenth century editions of these and similar stories have survived in chapbook form, and Nos. 368, 369 and 370 are typical of them.

Newbery does not seem himself to have been very actively interested in the chapbook market, but just as he unquestionably adopted the general format of his books from specimens of chapmen's wares in his native Salisbury, so, in his turn, he influenced their market and turned the attention of the publishers who supplied them to the popularity of stories and rhymes expressly composed for children. Nos. 382a and 385, although not really chapbooks, are included in this section as illustrations of the reverse process, namely the influence of chapmen on publishers of books for children.

368 THE CONQUEST OF FRANCE, WITH THE LIFE AND GLORIOUS ACTIONS OF EDWARD THE BLACK PRINCE ... [*Colophon :*] *Printed for and sold by Charles Bates ... [ca.* 1700 ?]. With a large woodcut on the title and two others in the text.

369 HISTORY OF THE MOST RENOWNED QUEEN ELIZABETH, AND HER GREAT FAVOURITE THE EARL OF ESSEX. IN TWO PARTS. A ROMANCE. 4to. *Printed by T. Norris, at the Looking-Glass on London Bridge, And Sold by S. Bates,* [? *ca.* 1700].

370 THE RENOWNED HISTORY (OR THE LIFE AND DEATH) OF GUY EARL OF WARWICK, CONTAINING HIS NOBLE EXPLOITS AND VICTORIES. 4to. *Printed by A. M. for C. Bates*, [*ca.* 1700]. With several large woodcuts in the text.

370a THE NOBLE AND RENOWNED HISTORY OF GUY, EARL OF WARWICK ... The Tenth Edition, 12mo. *Crowder*, 1759. Woodcut frontispiece (coloured), and numerous cuts in the text.

371 THE HISTORY OF GUY, EARL OF WARWICK. 8vo. *Nottingham : Walking Stationers*, 1796.

372 THE FAMOUS AND PLEASANT HISTORY OF PARISMUS, THE VALIANT AND RENOWNED PRINCE OF BOHEMIA. IN THREE PARTS ... Sm. 8vo. *Printed by Tho. Norton, at the Looking-Glass on London Bridge*, 1724.

373 ROMAN STORIES : OR, THE HISTORY OF THE SEVEN WISE MISTRESSES OF ROME : CONTAINING SEVEN DAYS' ENTERTAINMENT, IN MANY PLEASANT AND WITTY TALES, OR STORIES ... 12mo. *For J. Hodges, etc.*, 1754. With woodcut and printed title, and numerous cuts. With its lascivious and highly-coloured accounts of the peccadilloes of these wild mistresses, this would now be considered decidedly not a book for children.

374 THE ILLUSTRIOUS AND RENOWNED HISTORY OF THE SEVEN FAMOUS CHAMPIONS OF CHRISTENDOM. IN THREE PARTS. Ninth edition, 12mo. *For L. Hawes, etc.*, 1766. Numerous cuts in the text and frontispiece.

375 THE FAMOUS HISTORY OF THE VALIANT LONDON 'PRENTICE. 12mo. *Printed for the honourable Company of Walking Stationers*, [18*th century*]. Probably inspired by Dick Whittington, to which it bears a pale resemblance.

376 THE BRITISH CHAMPION ; OR HONOUR RE-
WARDED ... First edition, 24mo. *York :
Wilson, etc.*, [18th century]. Contains 7
stories with 43 cuts. J. Cresswell's Bewick
bookplate suggests that the cuts may be
Bewick's.

377 THE HOLY BIBLE ; CONTAINING THE OLD AND
NEW TESTAMENTS WITH THE APOCRYPHA,
DONE IN VERSE FOR THE BENEFIT OF WEAK
MEMORIES ... The Forty First Impression,
8vo. *Newcastle upon Tyne : Printed and
Sold by John White*, [18th century]. A great
favourite as the record of reprinting on the
title-page indicates. The Bible story is
condensed into about one thousand lines.
Deuteronomy and Ruth have six lines each,
Solomon's Song two lines more, but Joel,
Zephaniah and the three Epistles of John
have to put up with only three lines apiece.
Revelations is boiled down into 10 lines.
The author appears to have been one John
Bilcliff.

378 THE HISTORY OF THOMAS HICKATHRIFT. TWO
PARTS. 8vo. *Howard and Evans*, [18th
century].

379 THE FAMOUS HISTORY OF FRIAR BACON ...
PART I. *Printed in the Year* 1796.

380 THE HISTORY OF WAT TYLER AND JACK STRAW.
8vo. *Printed for the Travelling Stationers*,
[18th century].

381 THE HISTORY AND REAL ADVENTURES OF
ROBIN HOOD ... WRITTEN BY CAPT. C. JOHNSON
... 8vo. *Fox and Lemoine, etc.*, 1800.
Charles Johnson's histories of pirates and
highwaymen were fair game for the chapmen.

382 THE HISTORY OF ROBIN HOOD, CAPTAIN OF THE MERRY OUTLAWS OF SHERWOOD FOREST. *Alnwick : W. Davison, ca. 1820.*

382a ROBIN HOOD : BEING A COMPLETE HISTORY OF ALL THE NOTABLE AND MERRY EXPLOITS PERFORMED BY HIM AND HIS MEN ... 12mo. *Darton,* 1822. With 8 charming full-page coloured engravings.

383 THE HEROIC EXPLOITS OF VALENTINE AND ORSON. AN ANCIENT ROMANCE. 8vo. *Published by Kaygill, at his Circulating Library, Upper Rathbone Place . . .ca.* 1800.

384 THE RENOWNED HISTORY OF VALENTINE AND ORSON ... Newly corrected and revised. Adorned with cuts. 12mo. *Dublin : Cross, etc.,* 1802.

385 THE RENOWNED HISTORY OF VALENTINE AND ORSON. 12mo. *Tabart,* 1804.

386 THE LITTLE CARE KILLER, BEING A CHOICE VARIETY OF ANECDOTES, BON MOTS, ETC. . . . *Camden Town : T. Wallis, [ca.* 1810]. Three vols.

387 RICHARDSON'S JUVENILE CABINET. 16mo. *Derby : Richardson, ca.* 1820. Alphabets including " A—Apple Pie."

388 A COLLECTION OF EIGHTEEN PENNY CHAP-BOOKS. *Published at Banbury by J. G. Rusher, ca.* 1820. The titles include Dame Trot, Tom Thumb, London Jingles, Jack the Giant Killer, Cries of Banbury and London, Babes in the Wood, Cinderella, Dick Whittington, Robinson Crusoe, Mother Hubbard, Cock Robin, Jack and Jill, Jack Sprat. Fine copies.

389 THE AFFECTING HISTORY OF JANE SHORE. 8vo. *Alnwick : Davison, ca.* 1825.

390 THE AFFECTING HISTORY OF JANE SHORE.
8vo. *Derby* : *Richardson, ca.* 1845.

391 THE KNIFE-GRINDER'S BUDGET. 32mo. *Allman*
1829.

392 ENTERTAINING VIEWS. *Printed for the Booksellers, ca.* 1840.

SECTION II : **FAIRY STORIES**

Whether the mantle of ponderosity in research
remains with the Germans or passes to the
Americans or the Japanese, there is nothing more
certain than the eventual appearance of a *magnum
opus* on the origin and significance of the fairy-
tale. This side of the question is hardly germane
to our present purpose, although a passing
mention may be made of the fact that Hans
Andersen was an amateur and the brothers Grimm
were professionals in folk-lore.

The earliest appearance of any considerable
collection of fairy-tales in the western hemisphere
was the *Histoires ou Contes du temps passé* . . .
published in Paris in 1697, and is generally
attributed to Charles Perrault, a well-known
litterateur and a member of the *Academie
Française*. There can be little doubt, however,
that they were actually written by his son, Pierre,
a lad of eighteen or nineteen, who died three years
later. Space forbids a full discussion of the facts,
it must suffice to say that the privilege to publish
the book was granted to Pierre : that the
dedication of the first edition, to " mademoiselle,"
says : " on ne trouvera pas étrange qu'un enfant

ait pris plaisir à composer les Contes de ce Recueil ... " ; and that no claim by the father, nor attribution to him seems to be known in his lifetime.

The frontispiece of the original edition, a later version of which may be seen in our No. 393, not only includes the legend *Contes de ma M're L'Oie* (Tales of Mother Goose), the title under which these stories were first translated into English, but it also depicts a nurse telling stories to three children, while she is busy with a distaff. The three children are believed to be the daughter and two sons of Charles Perrault, the youngest of whom is the author of these stories.

All the early editions of Perrault are of the utmost rarity. Of the French and Dutch editions of 1697 the surviving copies are quite literally to be numbered on the fingers of one hand. A page for page reprint of 1700, and another of 1707, issued by the widow of the original publisher, Barbin, are almost equally rare.

The early English editions are even rarer than the French. It is, indeed, impossible to indicate with even approximate accuracy, the date of the first translation. The charming Nonesuch Press facsimile of 1925 was made from the earliest English edition yet known, which calls itself the " eleventh " and is dated 1719. We therefore consider ourselves fortunate in being able to include here two English eighteenth century editions of the book (Nos. 393 and 394), and also an early nineteenth century edition of Guy Miege's version.

The original editions of Perrault consist of eight stories, six—possibly seven—of which have retained an undimmed popularity down to our own times. The titles of the eight stories are :—

La belle au bois dormant (The Sleeping Beauty).
Le petit chaperon rouge (Red Riding Hood).
Barbe bleue (Blue Beard).
Le maître Chat (Puss in Boots).
Les Fées (Diamonds and Toads).
Rique a la Houppe (Riquet with the Tuft).
Le Petit Poucet (Hop o' my Thumb).
Cendrillon (Cinderella).

Although we have included under the Perrault section some editions of *Tom Thumb*, this is not strictly correct, for the story is an English one and probably of more ancient origin than Perrault's collection. It is included in this section because of its likeness to *Hop o' my Thumb*, and this and such stories as *Thumbelisa* bear witness to the similarity and wide range of the folk tale in all countries.

The western world also owes its knowledge of the " Arabian Nights " to a Frenchman—Antoine Galland (1646-1715). His translation of the original—*Les Milles et une nuits, contes arabes . . .* was published in Paris in twelve volumes between 1704 and 1708. An English translation from Galland's version was begun in 1704 and concluded in 1717, but no complete set appears now to be known.

The earliest versions for children were probably chapbooks similar to Nos. 413 and 418, and *Aladdin*, *Ali-Baba*, and *Sindbad* were probably adapted to this market as soon as they appeared in English. (See also No. 484).

The Comtesse d'Aulnoy (1650-1705) seems to have been the first to use the title " Fairy Tales " —*Contes des Feés*, 3 vols., 1698. They first appeared in English as the fourth volume (*Tales of the Fairies*) of her *Diverting Works*, in 1707. The stories of " Mother Bunch " are based on her work, which, in its turn, derives largely from *Il Pentamerone*.

PIERRE PERRAULT D'ARMANCOUR.

COLLECTED EDITIONS :—

393 THE HISTORIES OF PASSED TIMES, OR THE TALES OF MOTHER GOOSE. WITH MORALS. 2 vols., 12mo. *London printed; And sold at Brussels, By B. Le Francq, Book-seller,* 1785. An extremely fine copy, preserved in a half morocco box, of a very rare London edition, with frontispiece and 9 full-page engravings on thick paper. The title-pages in English and French, state that two new fairy-tales are added to this edition, namely " The Discreet Princess " and " The Widow and Her Two Daughters." This translation is the work of Robert Samber, the earliest surviving edition of which is the " third " of 1741.

394 TALES OF PAST TIMES ... 16mo. *York: Wilson, etc.,* 1797. With frontispiece and 8 cuts by Bewick : the first edition with these cuts.

395 HISTORIES, OR TALES OF PAST TIMES ... ENGLISHED BY G. M. GENT. 12mo. *Harris,* [*ca.* 1803]. This translation is probably the work of Guy Miege, a Swiss born at Lausanne in 1644, who probably died in

1718. The earliest surviving edition of his translation appears to be the " eleventh " of 1719, which was the original of the Nonesuch facsimile of 1925.

The interest of the edition shewn is that the exhibition also includes (No. 396) seven of the original drawings for the illustrations.

396 THE ORIGINAL DRAWINGS FOR SEVEN OF THE EIGHT VIGNETTES IN No. 397.

PERRAULT—SEPARATE STORIES :—

(THE BABES IN THE WOOD)

397 THE AFFECTING HISTORY OF THE CHILDREN IN THE WOOD. 32mo. *Hartford* [*Conn.*] : *Printed by J. Babcock*, 1796. An extremely rare American edition, not recorded by Rosenbach, who gives three books produced by Babcock, the earliest in 1798.

397a POLLOCK'S CHARACTERS AND SCENES IN THE CHILDREN IN THE WOOD. *Pollock, ca.* 1870. A coloured copy, complete with the book of words.

398 CHILDREN IN THE WOOD. 12mo. *Tabart*, 1807. Three hand-coloured copperplates.

(BLUEBEARD)

398a THE RENOWNED HISTORY OF BLUEBEARD ; with plates, taken from the splendid pageant represented at the Theatre-Royal, Drury Lane. 12mo. *Tabart*, 1809. The theatrical reference on the cover records an early example of the modern pantomime. The booklet also contains *Red-Riding-Hood*.

(CINDERELLA)

399 CINDERELLA, OR, THE LITTLE GLASS SLIPPER (THE FAIRY TALE OF). 12mo. *Innes,* [*ca.* 1820]. With a large folding coloured frontispiece with seven woodcuts.

400 CINDERELLA ; OR, THE LITTLE GLASS SLIPPER. 8vo. *Grant and Griffith, ca.* 1830. With vignette title and 14 half-page cuts, all coloured.

401 THE HISTORY OF CINDERELLA. *Printed for the Booksellers, ca.* 1840.

(PUSS IN BOOTS)

402 PUSS IN BOOTS. *ca.* 1840. An ingenious "perspective" toy book of a kind which has recently been revived ; the scene rises into place as the book is opened.

(RED RIDING HOOD)

402a TOO MUCH TALKING IS HURTFUL. *ca.* 1840. A "perspective" toy-book.

403 LITTLE RED RIDING HOOD. 4to. *John Cooke & Sons. ca.* 1850.

404 LILLIPUTIAN OPERA : RED RIDING HOOD : THE MUSIC BY ISIDORE DE SALLA. THE WORDS AND PICTURES BY R. ANDRÉ. Oblong 8vo. [*Nisbet, ca.* 1865].

(SLEEPING BEAUTY)

405 THE SLEEPING BEAUTY IN THE WOOD. A TALE. *Printed in the Year* 1796.

405a AWAKE, SLEEPING BEAUTY. *ca.* 1840. An ingenious perspective toy-book similar to 402 and 402a.

405b POLLOCK'S CHARACTERS AND SCENES IN THE SLEEPING BEAUTY IN THE WOOD ! OR, HARLE- QUIN AND THE MAGIC HORN. *Pollock, ca.* 1870. A coloured copy, complete with the book of words.

(Tom Thumb)

406 THE FAMOUS HISTORY OF TOM THUMB, WHERE-IN IS DECLARED, HIS MARVELLOUS ACTS OF MANHOOD, FULL OF WONDER AND MERRIMENT. Three parts, each in original woodcut wrappers, sm. 8vo. *Printed for the Booksellers, ca.* 1800.

407 THE HISTORY OF TOM THUMB. *Printed for the Booksellers, ca.* 1850. 8vo.

408 THE HISTORY OF TOM THUMB. 8vo. *Routledge, Warne and Routledge,* [1860].

---

409 THE PLEASANT AND DELIGHTFUL HISTORY OF JACK AND THE GIANTS. Two parts, 8vo. *Nottingham : for the Running Stationers* [18th century].

410 THE RENOWNED HISTORY OF JACK THE GIANT KILLER. *Derby : Thomas Richardson, ca.* 1820.

411 THE HISTORY OF JACK AND THE GIANTS. 8vo. *Kilmarnock : For the Booksellers,* [*ca.* 1825].

412 JACK THE GIANT KILLER. *Printed for the Booksellers, ca.* 1850.

(The Arabian Nights)

413 ALI BABA ; OR THE FORTY THIEVES . . . 12mo. *Wood and Cunningham,* [*ca.* 1820].

414 THE HISTORY OF ALI BABA, AND THE FORTY THIEVES. Sm. 8vo. *Carvalho,* [1835]. With 14 small woodcuts, two at the head of each page of text, all coloured.

415 MARCH'S PENNY LIBRARY. THE FORTY THIEVES. *ca.* 1850.

415a POLLOCK'S CHARACTERS AND SCENES IN THE FORTY THIEVES. *Pollock, ca.* 1870. A coloured copy, complete with the book of words.

416 ALI-BABA OR THE FORTY THIEVES. 8vo. *Marcus Ward, ca.* 1875. Printed in panorama form, one of the " Japanese Picture Stories." Mounted on linen.

417 40 THIEVES AND HOW TO CATCH THEM. A NEWLY INVENTED GAME. VERY FUNNY : EASY TO PLAY ... *Henry Reason's Copyright, ca.* 1880. From the designation of Cocia Houssain as Captain of the 40 Thieves, this was an evident attempt to use the appeal of the Arabian Nights. It is a Happy Families kind of game and the band is incongruous and anachronistic to a degree. It includes King Arthur, Who Stole a Peck of Meal to make a bag-pudding, Procrastination, Autolycus, Falstaff, Pym and Bardolph, The Dish who ran away with the Spoon, etc., and all are to be rounded up by eight police-constables.

418 THE HISTORY OF ALADDIN ; OR, THE WONDERFUL LAMP. 12mo. *Glasgow : Lumsden, ca.* 1830. Hand-coloured woodcuts.

419 MARCH'S PENNY LIBRARY. THE STORY OF ALADDIN AND HIS WONDERFUL LAMP. 8vo. *J. March, ca.* 1850.

419a POLLOCK'S CHARACTERS AND SCENES IN ALADDIN ; OR THE WONDERFUL LAMP. *Pollock, ca.* 1870. A coloured copy, complete with the book of words.

420 ALADDIN OR THE WONDERFUL LAMP. 8vo. *Marcus Ward & Co., ca.* 1875. In the same series and format as No. **416.**

(COUNTESSE D'AULNOY).

421 GRACIOSA AND PERCINET. 12mo. *Gainsborough*: *Mozley*, 1806. This and the following No. are evidence of the continued popularity of this story a century after its first appearance in English. Within a few years it was clearly worth while for one provincial publisher to reprint the text, albeit using the same cuts.

422 GRACIOSA AND PERCINET... Sq. 12mo. *Gainsborough*: *Mozley, ca.* 1810.

423 THE WHITE CAT. 24mo. *Marshall*, 1819. With 6 full-page coloured cuts.

424 THE ROYAL FAIRY TALES; TAKEN FROM THE MOST POLITE AUTHORS... 12mo. *Dublin*: *Cross*, 1801. Six fairy stories translated from the Countess d'Aulnoy, among them The Yellow Dwarf and The White Cat.

---

425 THE HISTORY OF THE TALES OF THE FAIRIES. NEWLY DONE FROM THE FRENCH... DEDICATED TO THE LADIES OF GREAT BRITAIN. First edition, sm. 8vo. *Printed and sold by D. Peatt*... 1721. Extremely rare; this appears to be the only recorded copy. Woodcut frontispiece. The stories are Graciosa and Pertinet; The Blew-Bird, and Florina; Prince Avenant; The King of the Peacocks; Prince Nonpareil; and the Orange-Tree.

426 JACK AND THE BEANSTALK. *Edinburgh*: *W. P. Nimmo, ca.* 1860.

427 THE HISTORY OF MOTHER TWADDLE AND THE MARVELLOUS ATCHIEVMENTS OF HER SON JACK. BY B.A.T. First edition, 12mo. *Harris*, 1807. This is the complete story of Jack and the Beanstalk under another name. With 13 coloured engravings and engraved title and text.

428 MOTHER GOOSE AND THE GOLDEN EGG. Cr. 8vo. *Catnach, ca.* 1840. This is The Goose that laid the Golden Eggs.

429 GRANDPAPA EASY'S NEW MOTHER GOOSE AND THE GOLDEN EGGS. *Dean & Co., ca.* 1840.

430 TABART'S COLLECTION OF POPULAR STORIES FOR THE NURSERY ... First edition, 3 vols., 12mo. *Tabart,* 1804. With 18 engravings, many of them coloured, one leaf of text defective. Includes all the old favourites from Perrault, d'Aulnoy, etc.

431 MOTHER BUNCH'S FAIRY TALES. PUBLISHED FOR THE AMUSEMENT OF ALL THOSE LITTLE MASTERS AND MISSES WHO, BY DUTY TO THEIR PARENTS, AND OBEDIENCE TO THEIR SUPERIORS, AIM AT BECOMING GREAT LORDS AND LADIES. 12mo. *Harris,* 1802. Although described by Darton as a generic name " Mother Bunch " usually contained the same stories taken from d'Aulnoy and others.

432 MOTHER BUNCH'S FAIRY TALES ... Sq. 24mo. *Glasgow : Lumsden, ca.* 1810.

433 THE CELEBRATED TALES OF MOTHER BUNCH ... Sm. 8vo. *Harris, ca.* 1825. This edition includes Jack and the Beanstalk.

434 THE ADVENTURES OF A SILVER PENNY. INCLUDING MANY SECRET ANECDOTES OF LITTLE MISSES AND MASTERS BOTH GOOD AND NAUGHTY. First edition, 12mo. *E. Newbery,* [1787]. With a woodcut frontispiece and a vignette to each chapter. Extremely scarce. Welsh, p. 306, records it only from an advertisement.

435 CHOISEUL (COMTESSE DE). THE RETURN OF THE FAIRIES. First edition, sm. 8vo. *Dublin : John Cumming,* [1827].

435a THE FAIRING ; OR, A GOLDEN TOY FOR CHILDREN OF ALL SIZES AND DENOMINATIONS, IN WHICH THEY MAY SEE ALL THE FUN OF THE FAIR, AND AT HOME BE AS HAPPY AS IF THEY WERE THERE ... *W. Osborne and T. Griffin* ... 1782. This includes Dick Whittington and Puss in Boots.

436 THE ANCIENT HISTORY OF WHITTINGTON AND HIS CAT. 12mo. *Darton*, [*ca.* 1820]. Engraved title and 3 other engravings.

436a POLLOCK'S CHARACTERS AND SCENES IN WHITTINGTON AND HIS CAT, OR HARLEQUIN LORD MAYOR OF LONDON. *Pollock, ca.* 1870. A coloured copy complete with the book of words.

437 ELIZA LUCY LEONARD. THE RUBY RING ; OR THE TRANSFORMATIONS. Second edition, sq. 12mo. *Hailes*, 1820. With 8 charming full-page coloured engravings.

438 NURSE DANDLEM'S LITTLE REPOSITORY OF GREAT INSTRUCTION, CONTAINING THE SURPRISING ADVENTURES OF LITTLE WAKE WILFUL, AND HIS DELIVERANCE FROM THE GIANT GRUMBOLUMBO ... FOR THE SOLE AMUSEMENT OF THE CHICKABIDDY GENERATION. 24mo. *Glasgow : Lumsden*, [*ca.* 1810]. With 14 engravings printed in red.

439 THE FAIRY SPECTATOR ; OR, THE INVISIBLE MONITOR. BY MRS. TEACHWELL AND HER FAMILY. First edition, sm. 8vo. *Marshall*, 1789. Engraved frontispiece.

440 THE VISIONS OF HERON ; THE HERMIT OF THE SILVER ROCK ; OR, A JOURNEY TO THE MOON ... First edition, 24mo. *Roberts*, 1777. With 7 full-page engravings.

441 WILLIAM TELL, OR THE PATRIOT OF SWITZER-
LAND. BY FLORIAN. *And* HOFER, THE
TYROLESE. BY THE AUTHOR OF " CLAUDINE,"
ETC. First edition, sm. 8vo. *Harris*, 1823.
With coloured engraved title and 22 charm-
ing half-page coloured engravings.

442 WISHING ; OR, THE FISHERMAN AND HIS
WIFE ; A JUVENILE POEM. BY A LADY.
12mo. *Newman,* [*ca.* 1825]. With a coloured
frontispiece and 24 coloured woodcuts.

SECTION III : FABLES

443 AESOP'S FABLES, WITH HIS LIFE, MORALS AND
REMARKS. FITTED FOR THE MEANEST CAPACI-
TIES. The ninth edition, with large additions,
sm. 8vo. *For R. Ware, C. Hitch, and J.
Hodges,* 1747. With a woodcut frontispiece
and a vignette to each fable.

444 FABLES OF THE WISE AESOP, WITH INSTRUC-
TIVE APPLICATIONS. THE LILLIPUTIAN LIBRARY
OR GULLIVER'S MUSEUM . . . VOL. III. First
edition, sq. 16mo. *Domville,* [*ca.* 1760].
Woodcut illustrations. The Advertisement
adds " N.B. This work is printed in such a
manner (like the Spectators) that one volume
does not depend upon another ; so that little
Masters or Misses may be supplied with any
one or more volumes . . ."

445 SELECT FABLES OF ESOP AND OTHER FABULISTS
Cr. 8vo. *Birmingham* : *John Baskerville,*
1761. Engraved title and frontispiece, and
numerous small engravings. The pictures
make it possible that this finely printed
edition may have been produced with at
least one eye on the juvenile public.

446 THE AMUSING INSTRUCTOR ; OR, TALES AND FABLES IN PROSE AND VERSE FOR THE IMPROVEMENT OF YOUTH. First edition, 12mo. *F. Newbery*, 1777. Philander, a rich gentleman, sick of dissipation and amusement, retires to the country to devote himself to benevolence, taking as his motto " Virtue alone is happiness below." He entertains each Monday six young gentlemen—Master Steady, Master Featherbrain, Master Speakwell, etc.—and each Thursday six young ladies—Miss Allgood, Miss Prattle, Miss Haughty, etc. After one of them has told a story or recited a poem, the remainder of the visit is devoted to the study of the sciences in which each pupil speaks his piece in nauseating sententiousness interlarded with piety.

447 TICKLEPITCHER (T.). TALES AND FABLES FROM THE WORKS OF EMINENT WRITERS . . . WITH 59 PICTURES BY P. VAN GRAVE. First edition, 12mo. *Marshall*, [*ca.* 1788].

448 ENTERTAINING FABLES FOR THE INSTRUCTION OF CHILDREN. First edition, 24mo. *Evans*, [*c.* 1785]. With frontispiece and numerous cuts in the text.

449 SELECT TALES AND FABLES, WITH PRUDENTIAL MAXIMS AND OTHER LITTLE LESSONS OF MORALITY . . . THE WHOLE EMBELLISH'D WITH THREESCORE ORIGINAL DESIGNS . . . NEATLY ENGRAV'D ON COPPER PLATES BY B. COLE. First edition, 2 vols. in 1, fcap. 8vo. *Wingrave*, [*18th century*]. Extremely rare. The plates are after Samuel Wale.

450 FABLES IN PROSE AND VERSE. PART I. 24mo. *For the assigns of J. Newbery and T. Carnan*, N.D.

451 SELECT FABLES FOR CHILDREN. First edition, sm. 8vo. *Derby : Richardson,* [*ca.* 1820]. With coloured title and frontispiece, and numerous cuts in the text.

452 JEFFERYS TAYLOR. AESOP IN RHYME, WITH SOME ORIGINALS. Second edition, 8vo. *Baldwin, Cradock and Jay,* 1823.

453 FABLES OF LA FONTAINE, WITH MOVING PICTURES. 8vo. *S.P.C.K., ca.* 1875. Printed *in* Bavaria, possibly an early Meggendorfer.

SECTION IV : MORAL TALES

(*a*) *Books acknowledged by their Authors :*—

ARNAUD BERQUIN (1747-1791) is not the originator of the moral tale, which probably originates in Rousseauism, the influence of which may be traced widely in the present exhibition, in the Robinsonades, in Day and Edgeworth, and never very far in the background of the books published by the Newberys and their like. Berquin, however, is typical of the writers of moral tales, and his popularity was as prevalent in England as in France. It is significant that he produced French versions of *Sandford and Merton* and *The Little Grandison.*

454 L'AMI DES ENFANS, PAR M. BERQUIN. Janvier 1782, No. 1 [to Décembre 1782, No. 12]. *A Paris, Au Bureau de l'Ami des Enfans . . .* [later, *Au Bureau du Journal*] . . . 1782. The first twelve of the twenty-four monthly parts; 10 are first editions.

455 THE CHILDREN'S FRIEND ; CONSISTING OF APT TALES, SHORT DIALOGUES, AND MORAL DRAMAS, ALL INTENDED TO ENGAGE ATTEN-

TION, CHERISH FEELING, AND INCULCATE VIRTUE IN THE RISING GENERATION. TRANSLATED BY THE REV. MARK ANTHONY MEILAN. First English edition, 24 vols. in 12, 16mo. *Printed for the Translator, and to be had of John Stockdale*, 1786. Dedication copy, with a full-page MS. copperplate inscription from the translator dated 1787. Two printed lists of subscribers. An exceedingly rare and very charming complete set of the first English translation. Darton quotes the date wrongly as 1783. The popularity of the book was as great in England as in France, and Newbery's abridgement of it, with the title *The Looking-Glass for the Mind*, had an enormous sale ; an edition of it appeared as late as 1885.

456 THE LOOKING-GLASS FOR THE MIND ; OR, INTELLECTUAL MIRROR . . . CHIEFLY TRANSLATED FROM THAT MUCH ADMIRED WORK *L'Ami des Enfans*. Seventh edition, 8vo. *E. Newbery*, 1798. Newbery's version first appeared in 1792. The cuts are by John Bewick. The editor of this version was the prolific Mr. Cooper.

The industrious TAYLORS OF ONGAR included five members engaged in the production of books for children—the father, Isaac, two daughters Ann and Jane, and two sons Isaac and Jefferys. The father, originally an engraver and afterwards a Nonconformist pastor, wrote didactically on geography and history. Jefferys produced two prose works and a rhymed version of Aesop for children, while Isaac the younger, besides writing himself, illustrated the books of his more famous sisters.

They began, modestly enough, when Ann was sixteen and Jane a year younger, by submitting an acceptable poetical solution of the puzzles in *Minor's Pocket Book* for 1798, which won the first prize and brought them to the notice of the publishers, Darton and Harvey. After contributing regularly to " Minor's " for some years the sisters, with the aid of contributions from father and brother Isaac, Bernard Barton and Adelaide O'Keefe, produced *Original Poems for Infant Minds* (first edition 1804-5, 30th edition, 1875, definitive edition, edited with an introduction by E. V. Lucas, 1903). This included one immortal poem *Twinkle, Twinkle Little Star*, and one even more famous in its day, *My Mother*. The latter was first printed separately in 1807 with illustrations from drawings by brother Isaac, and was subsequently reprinted in a multiplicity of varying forms and editions. No. 457 comprises the original manuscript and drawings for the first separate edition of the poem. We also shew a representative selection of other works by members of the family.

457 ANN TAYLOR. MY MOTHER. A POEM. EMBELLISHED WITH DESIGNS. BY A LADY. *ca.* 1807. The original holograph manuscript entirely in the author's hand and with the nine original pencil drawings by her brother Isaac. Lady Hamilton is said to have sat for these drawings.

458 MY MOTHER . . . *Fairburn, ca.* 1820. The description " Second Edition " on the wrapper and title are completely irrelevant. Liberties have been taken with the text and the order of the verses changed.

459 MY MOTHER. *ca.* 1850. Each verse printed on a separate card. Considerable further liberties are here taken with the text.

460 ANN TAYLOR. SIGNOR TOPSY-TURVY'S WONDERFUL MAGIC LANTERN; OR, THE WORLD TURNED UPSIDE DOWN. First edition, sq. 12mo. *Tabart*, 1810. *Cf* Nos. 736 to 739. With 24 full-page engravings.

461 ANNE AND JANE TAYLOR. HYMNS FOR INFANT MINDS. First edition, 12mo. *Conder*, 1810. Almost as famous in its day as *Original Poems*. In this copy, in an old hand, the work of each of the two authors is indicated in pencil. Formerly the property of James Montgomery who has written on the fly-leaves a poem " To Ann and Jane."

462 REV. ISAAC TAYLOR. SCENES OF BRITISH WEALTH . . . First edition, sm. 8vo. *Harris*, 1823. On the fore-edge, completely concealed by the marbling, is a fine painting of a street-scene. The book itself is illustrated with a folding coloured map and 84 small coloured engravings.

463 JEFFERYS TAYLOR. AESOP IN RHYME. Second edition, sm. 8vo. *Baldwin*, 1823.

MARY ELLIOTT (*née* Belson) belongs to the same period as the Taylors and her works were equally popular with theirs. She began to write in the early years of the century and her popularity continued into the 'fifties.

464 GRATEFUL TRIBUTES ; OR RECOLLECTIONS OF INFANCY. First edition, sq. 12mo. *Darton*, 1811. This is an attempt to cash in on the popularity of Ann Taylor's " My Mother," with similar verses on other members of the family.

465 TALES FOR GIRLS AND BOYS. First collected edition, 12mo. *Darton, ca.* 1820. Each of the four stories has a folding frontispiece and separate pagination.

466 FLOWERS OF INSTRUCTION : OR, FAMILIAR SUBJECTS IN VERSE. First edition, sm. 8vo. *Darton*, [1820].

467 AMUSEMENT FOR LITTLE GIRLS. First edition, sq. 12mo. *Darton, ca.* 1825. With coloured engraved title and four charming coloured engravings.

468 THE ROSE, CONTAINING ORIGINAL POEMS FOR YOUNG PEOPLE. First edition, sm. 8vo. *Darton, ca.* 1823. With 12 rather crudely coloured copperplates of children's games, including cricket.

469 PLAIN THINGS FOR LITTLE FOLKS. First edition, sm. 8vo. *Darton, ca.* 1825. With 24 half-page engravings.

DOROTHY and MARY JANE KILNER were sisters living in the country at Maryland Point, a village whose initials served as a pseudonym for Dorothy. Jane also wrote as " S. S." They were great friends of Mrs. Trimmer. Both sisters were prolific and popular writers. Dorothy lived to the age of 81.

470 THE VILLAGE SCHOOL ; OR, A COLLECTION OF ENTERTAINING HISTORIES ... First edition, 2 vols., 12mo. *Marshall, ca.* 1785.

471 THE LIFE AND PERAMBULATION OF A MOUSE. First edition, 2 vols., 12mo. *Marshall, ca.* 1790.

472 MEMOIRS OF A PEG-TOP. BY THE AUTHOR OF ADVENTURES OF A PINCUSHION. First edition 12mo. *Marshall*, [*ca.* 1790]. The first issue, with an engraved title.

473 MEMOIRS OF A PEG-TOP. BY THE AUTHOR OF ADVENTURES OF A PINCUSHION. *Marshall*, [*ca.* 1790]. A later edition, entirely reset, with printed title and woodcut illustrations.

474 THE ADVENTURES OF A PINCUSHION, DESIGNED CHIEFLY FOR THE USE OF YOUNG LADIES. First edition (?), 12mo. *Marshall*, [*ca.* 1790]. The first edition may have had an engraved title.

THOMAS DAY (1748 to 1789). Little needs to be said here of this curious person, whose eccentricities have been widely publicized. Judging by the comparative frequency of reprints, *Little Jack* seems to have been a more general favourite with the young than *Sandford and Merton*—perhaps because it is so much shorter.

475 THE HISTORY OF SANDFORD AND MERTON; ABRIDGED FROM THE ORIGINAL. 12mo. *Wallis & Newbery*. Originally published in three volumes (1783-9). This abridgement appeared originally over John Wallis's imprint in 1790.

476 THE FORSAKEN INFANT; OR ENTERTAINING HISTORY OF LITTLE JACK. *Gainsborough*: *Mozley*, 1796. The story originally appeared in Stockdale's *Children's Miscellany* in 1788 and afterwards separately by the same publisher. The cuts in the present edition are by John Bewick and this is their first appearance.

477 THE HISTORY OF LITTLE JACK. EMBELLISHED WITH 22 BEAUTIFUL PRINTS, CUT BY BEWICK. *Stockdale*, 1800. An entirely different series of cuts from those in No. 476.

478 THE FORSAKEN INFANT ; OR, ENTERTAINING HISTORY OF LITTLE JACK. *Derby : Mozley*, 1807. The cuts of the 1796 edition are still used here.

479 THE HISTORY OF LITTLE JACK, WHO WAS SUCKLED BY A GOAT. *Derby : Richardson*, ca. 1820.

480 THE HISTORY OF LITTLE JACK. *Chiswick : C. Whittingham*, 1820. The cuts are mostly " modernized " versions of those of Bewick in No. 477.

The REVEREND JOHN TRUSLER (1735-1820), an eccentric cleric, studied medicine, moralised Hogarth, and opened a bookselling business, in addition to compiling several rather heavy-handed books for children.

481 PROVERBS EXEMPLIFIED ; AND ILLUSTRATED BY PICTURES FROM REAL LIFE . . . DESIGNED AS A SUCCESSION-BOOK TO AESOP'S FABLES. First edition, sm. 8vo. *Author, etc.*, 1790. " With 50 woodcuts from the graver of John Bewick, most of them being tokens of considerable ability."—Hugo, No. (43).

482 THE PROGRESS OF MAN AND SOCIETY. ILLUS- TRATED BY UPWARDS OF 120 CUTS. OPENING THE EYES, AND UNFOLDING THE MIND OF YOUTH GRADUALLY. First edition, 8vo. *Author, etc.*, 1791. " With marvellously clever cuts by John Bewick."—Hugo, No. (59). A fine copy.

The REVEREND MR. COOPER was almost exclusively a Newbery author, and evidence of his work will be found elsewhere in this catalogue, especially as translator and editor of Newbery's edition of Berquin (No. 456).

483 THE BLOSSOMS OF MORALITY. INTENDED FOR THE AMUSEMENT AND INSTRUCTION OF YOUNG LADIES AND GENTLEMEN. First edition, sm. 8vo. *E. Newbery*, 1789.

484 THE ORIENTAL MORALIST OR THE BEAUTIES OF THE ARABIAN NIGHTS' ENTERTAINMENTS. First edition, sm. 8vo. *E. Newbery*, [*ca.* 1790].

ANNA LETITIA BARBAULD (1743-1825), *née* Aikin, sister of and collaborator with the doctor-poet, was a famous 'blue-stocking' praised by Dr. Johnson. She and her husband kept a school at Palgrave in Suffolk. Her first book for children was the famous *Lessons*, 1780, and the second, *Hymns in Prose*, 1781, of which a later edition is shewn here.

485 HYMNS IN PROSE, FOR CHILDREN ... 12mo. *Derby* : *Richardson*, 1834.

486 THE THREE CAKES ; OR, HARRY, PETER, AND BILLY. A TALE IN VERSE. First edition, sm. 8vo. *Harris*, 1824.

MARY MARTHA SHERWOOD (1775-1851), *née* Butt, was of sterner, albeit coarser stuff than Mrs. Barbauld. She believed that " all children are by nature evil " and must be forced into good behaviour. Like so many writers for children, she could churn out her books without ceasing—

the Cambridge Bibliography lists nearly sixty titles between 1793 and 1851. She was strongly against fairy-tales.

487 THE HISTORY OF LITTLE HENRY AND HIS BEARER. First edition, fcap. 8vo. *Wellington*: *Houlston*, 1814. Written in India under the influence of Henry Martyn, the great missionary, this is the classic missionary story for children. Its successors are innumerable.

488 EMANCIPATION. First edition, fcap. 8vo. *Wellington* : *Houlston*, 1829. With a printed advertisement leaf of Mrs. Sherwood's school.

SARAH TRIMMER (1741-1810), *née* Kirby, belied her married name, for opinions more forthright or more forcibly expressed than hers it would be difficult to imagine. She thought it positively sinful to allow children to read fairy-tales. *Cinderella*, for example, she thought one of the worst books ever written for children, depicting the vilest of human passions, including " envy, jealousy, a dislike to mothers-in-law and half-sisters, vanity, a love of dress, etc., etc." She was rather a writer about children than for them, but one classic came from her pen—*The History of the Robins*.

489 FABULOUS HISTORIES DESIGNED FOR THE INSTRUCTION OF CHILDREN, RESPECTING THEIR TREATMENT OF ANIMALS. Second edition, sm. 8vo. *Longman, etc.*, 1786. This typically forbidding title conceals the charming and popular *History of the Robins*. The first edition appeared earlier in the same year.

490 MRS. PILKINGTON (1766-1839). THE ASIATIC PRINCESS. First edition, 2 vols. in 1, 12mo. *Vernon and Wood & E. Newbery*, 1800.

490a MRS. PINCHARD. THE BLIND CHILD, OR ANECDOTES OF THE WYNDHAM FAMILY. WRITTEN FOR THE USE OF YOUNG PEOPLE. BY A LADY. First edition, fcap. 8vo. *E. Newbery*, 1791.

491 [PINCHARD (MRS.)]. THE TWO COUSINS, A MORAL STORY, FOR THE USE OF YOUNG PERSONS . . . BY THE AUTHOR OF THE BLIND CHILD . . . First edition, 8vo. *E. Newbery*, 1798.

492 VAUX (F. B.). HENRY ; A STORY, INTENDED FOR LITTLE BOYS AND GIRLS, FROM FIVE TO SEVEN YEARS OLD. First edition, fcap. 8vo. *Darton*, [1815].

493 [WEST (MRS.)]. THE SORROWS OF SELFISH-NESS ; OR, THE HISTORY OF MISS RICHMORE. BY MRS. PRUDENTIA HOMESPUN. First edition, 8vo. *Harris*, 1812.

494 [KENDALL (E. A.)]. KEEPER'S TRAVELS IN SEARCH OF HIS MASTER. First edition, 12mo. *E. Newbery*, 1798. Exceedingly scarce. Welsh cites only the second edition, 1799.

495 [FENN (LADY ELEANOR)] (1743-1813). COB-WEBS TO CATCH FLIES ; OR, DIALOGUES IN SHORT SENTENCES. First edition, 2 vols. *Marshall*, [ca. 1783]. The author wrote under the pseudonyms "Mrs. Teachwell" and "Mrs. Lovechild." Her husband, Sir John Fenn, was the first editior of *The Paston Letters*.

496 H. JESSEY *and* A. CHEAT. A LOOKING-GLASS FOR CHILDREN. BEING A NARRATIVE OF GOD'S GRACIOUS DEALINGS WITH SOME LITTLE CHILDREN ... TO WHICH IS ADDED MANY OTHER POEMS VERY SUITABLE. AS ALSO SOME ELEGIES ON DEPARTED FRIENDS ... ALL NOW FAITHFULLY GATHERED TOGETHER ... BY H. P. Third edition, 12mo. *For Robert Boulter*, 1673.

497 THE REV. THOMAS WHITE. A LITTLE BOOK FOR LITTLE CHILDREN : WHEREIN ARE SET DOWN SEVERAL DIRECTIONS FOR LITTLE CHILDREN AND SEVERAL REMARKABLE STORIES BOTH ANCIENT AND MODERN OF LITTLE CHILDREN. DIVERS WHEREOF ARE OF THOSE WHO ARE RECENTLY DECEASED. 12mo. *Parkhurst*, 1702. A gruesome book, which includes several of the more harrowing stories from Foxe's *Book of Martyrs*, and recommends children to eschew " Ballads and foolish books " but to " Read often Treatises of Death, and Hell, and Judgement ..."

(b) Anonymous.

A comparison between the text of *The Conjurer* (No. 498) and *The Valentine's Gift* (No. 499) shews with unmistakeable clarity the service that Newbery performed. His " moral tales " may strike the modern child as forbidding, and one may pity a generation of children for whom this kind of story was the best that could be found ; these children were written down to, the tone of the books is clearly a product of what their elders thought they would like and shows little or no consciousness of the child's point of view.

Newbery and his competitors and successors were in no doubt that the only possible adornment for a children's tale was a very pointed moral; nevertheless, their books were an enormous improvement on anything that had gone before, indeed the difference is of kind rather than of degree.

Moreover, modern criticism of the books and their publishers should not be overweighted. They must be considered in relation to their social background. The dresses of children of the period, their method of deportment, education and general upbringing all combine to display the fact that they were regarded as miniature adults. Hence, for example, the adaptation of Gulliver, Robinson Crusoe, and their like for youthful readers, and the evidence that Aesop, the early bestiaries, and the *Gesta Romanorum* were given to children to read, all point to this fact.

The very remarkable insight of Newbery confronts one at every turn. The tiny format of his books, their attractive clothing, and their excellent print and paper, set a standard which is seldom surpassed even to-day, and to the charm of his titles and the art of his invention of names for his authors the present catalogue pays generous tribute.

498 THE CONJUROR; OR METAMORPHOSES OF PRIDE AND HUMILITY: AN HUMOROUS POLITICAL TALE: INTENDED AS A MORAL ENTERTAINMENT FOR BOTH SEXES IN THEIR YOUTH ... First edition, sq. 12mo. *Printed for*

John Ryland, Engraver, J. Wilkie, [a third imprint erased from the plate], ca. 1760. With engraved title and frontispiece and 22 engraved plates. An amusingly written tale in verse of a conjurer (or wizard) who interchanged the wives of a cobbler and a knight. Coarsely written and much too strong meat for children ; in fact more of an immoral than a moral tale.

499 THE VALENTINE'S GIFT ; OR, A PLAN TO ENABLE CHILDREN OF ALL SIZES AND DENOMINATIONS TO BEHAVE WITH HONOUR, INTEGRITY AND HUMANITY. VERY NECESSARY IN A TRADING NATION. TO WHICH IS ADDED, SOME ACCOUNT OF OLD ZIGZAG ... *Printed for the Booksellers* ... [*ca.* 1765].

500 FILIAL DUTY, RECOMMENDED AND ENFORC'D, BY A VARIETY OF INSTRUCTIVE AND ENTERTAINING STORIES OF CHILDREN ... First edition, 12mo. *F. Newbery,* [*ca.* 1770].

501 THE LITTLE FEMALE ORATORS ; OR, NINE EVENINGS' ENTERTAINMENT .. Second edition, 12mo. *Carnan,* 1773. Originally published 1770.

502 THE FRIENDS ; OR, THE HISTORY OF BILLY FREEMAN AND TOMMY TRUELOVE ... First edition, 32mo. *Marshall, ca.* 1775.

503 THE HAPPY FAMILY ; OR, MEMOIRS OF MR. AND MRS. NORTON. INTENDED TO SHOW THE DELIGHTFUL EFFECTS OF FILIAL OBEDIENCE. First edition, 12mo. *Marshall,* [*ca.* 1775].

504 JUVENILE TRIALS FOR ROBBING ORCHARDS, TELLING FIBS, AND OTHER HEINOUS OFFENCES. BY MASTER TOMMY LITTLETON. First edition (?), 16mo. *T. Carnan,* 1776. Extremely scarce : the earliest edition given

by Welsh is 1781. He calls it " A delightful book in which children become judge and jury to try juvenile offences." The frontispiece shows the court in session and there are numerous charming cuts, one shewing juvenile Bow Street Runners.

505 TEA-TABLE DIALOGUES, BETWEEN A GOVERNESS AND MISS SENSIBLE ... Sq. 12mo. *Carnan*, 1779. Extremely rare. Welsh quotes it only from the entry at Stationers' Hall in 1771.

506 VIRTUE IN A COTTAGE ; OR, A MIRROR FOR CHILDREN IN HUMBLE LIFE. First edition, 16mo. *Marshall*, [*ca.* 1780]. Compare this with No. 507.

507 VIRTUE IN A VILLAGE ; OR, A LOOKING-GLASS FOR CHILDREN IN HUMBLE LIFE. 16mo. *Printed for the Booksellers* ... 1795. This is a barefaced piracy of No. 506. The alteration of a single word in the title is matched by the changing of the names of characters— Sally Bark to Sally Sweet, Mrs. Flight to Mrs. Placid, etc., otherwise the stories are word for word identical, with the exception that the later version has some rather irrelevant sets of verses tacked on at the end.

508 THE HOLIDAY PRESENT CONTAINING ANECDOTES OF MR. AND MRS. JENNET, AND THEIR LITTLE FAMILY ... Second edition, 12mo. *Marshall*, [*ca.* 1780].

509 THE TRIUMPH OF GOODNATURE, EXHIBITED IN THE HISTORY OF MASTER HARRY FAIRBORN AND MASTER TRUEWORTH. INTERSPERSED WITH TALES AND FABLES. First edition, 16mo. *E. Newbery*, [*ca.* 1780].

510 THE RENOWNED HISTORY OF GILES GINGER-
BREAD : A LITTLE BOY WHO LIVED ON
LEARNING. 32mo. *Carnan*, 1782. The
Bodleian copy is "Newbery & Carnan," 1769,
but the original date of publication was 1766.
" Giles Gingerbread " was as great a favourite in its day as " Goody Two-Shoes."
Nichols in his *Literary Anecdotes* says it was
written by Griffith Jones but Welsh had a
lingering suspicion that Goldsmith had a
hand in it.

511 JEMIMA PLACID ; OR, THE ADVANTAGE OF
GOOD-NATURE . . . *Marshall*, *ca.* 1785.

512 THE RATIONAL DAME ; OR, HINTS TOWARDS
SUPPLYING PRATTLE FOR CHILDREN. *Marshall*,
[*ca.* 1790].

513 ANECDOTES FOR CHILDREN. COLLECTED FROM
THE BEST AUTHORS AND RECENT OCCUR-
RENCES. First edition, sm. 8vo. *Darton &
Harvey*, 1796. A most interesting copy ; on
the back of the frontispiece is a contemporary
drawing shewing the position and plan of
Darton's shop in Gracechurch Street.

514 THE HISTORY OF THE GOODVILLE FAMILY ;
OR, THE REWARDS OF VIRTUE AND FILIAL
DUTY. First edition, sq. 12mo. *York :
Wilson & Spence*, *ca.* 1796.

515 THE HISTORY OF SOLOMON SERIOUS AND HIS
DOG POMPEY, CONTAINING MANY PLEASING
PARTICULARS OF SOLOMON'S LIFE, HIS RAPID
PROGRESS IN LEARNING, HIS WONDERFUL
DISCOVERIES WITH THE MICROSCOPE. First
edition, 12mo. *Fairburn*, 1797. (See also
No. 558).

516 THE HISTORY OF A PIN, AS RELATED BY ITSELF,
INTERSPERSED WITH A VARIETY OF ANEC-
DOTES . . . BY THE AUTHOR OF THE BROTHERS.
First edition, sm. 8vo. *E. Newbery*, 1798.

517 THREE DAYS CHAT. DIALOGUES BETWEEN YOUNG LADIES AND THEIR GOVERNESSES. First edition, 12mo. *Gainsborough : Mozley,* [*ca.* 1798].

518 THE SILVER THIMBLE. BY THE AUTHOR OF INSTRUCTIVE TALES. First edition, 12mo. *E. Newbery,* 1799.

519 THE RATIONAL EXHIBITION FOR CHILDREN. First edition, sm. 8vo. *Darton,* 1800.

519a THE RATIONAL EXHIBITION. Sm. 8vo. *Darton,* 1824. An illustrated reprint of 519.

520 THE HAPPY FAMILY : OR, WINTER EVENING'S EMPLOYMENT . . . BY A FRIEND OF YOUTH. WITH CUTS BY BEWICK. *York : Wilson & Spence,* 1801.

521 THE SECOND CHAPTER OF ACCIDENTS AND REMARKABLE EVENTS : CONTAINING CAUTION AND INSTRUCTION FOR CHILDREN. First edition, 12mo. *Darton and Harvey,* 1801.

522 A PRESENT FOR A LITTLE GIRL. First edition, sm. 8vo. *Darton and Harvey,* 1802. With numerous charming woodcuts.

522a A PRESENT FOR A LITTLE GIRL. *Darton,* 1808. A reprint of No. 522, with new illustrations.

523 SUMMER RAMBLES, OR CONVERSATIONS, IN-STRUCTIVE AND ENTERTAINING FOR THE USE OF CHILDREN . . . BY A LADY. First edition, 2 vols. in 1, sm. 8vo. *Lloyd,* 1801.

524 TAKE YOUR CHOICE : OR, THE DIFFERENCE BETWEEN VIRTUE AND VICE, SHOWN IN OPPOSITE CHARACTERS. First edition, sm. 8vo. *Harris,* 1802.

525 A PRESENT FOR A LITTLE BOY. First edition, sm. 8vo. *Darton*, 1805. With coloured vignette title and 25 full and half-page coloured engravings.

526 A PRESENT FOR A LITTLE BOY. *Darton*, 1830. A reprint of No. 525, with a new series of illustrations.

527 THE MAGIC LANTERN, OR, AMUSING AND INSTRUCTIVE EXHIBITIONS FOR YOUNG PEOPLE ... First edition, sm. 8vo. *Tabart*, [1806].

528 A PUZZLE FOR A CURIOUS GIRL. 12mo. *Tabart*, 1806.

529 THE TRUE HISTORY OF A LITTLE BOY WHO CHEATED HIMSELF. FOUNDED ON FACT. BY A YOUNG NAVAL OFFICER. First edition, 12mo. *Tabart*, 1809. With 12 full-page coloured engravings.

530 MY FRIEND, OR INCIDENTS IN LIFE, FOUNDED ON TRUTH. A TRIFLE FOR CHILDREN. First edition, 12mo. *Darton*, 1810. 16 hand-coloured engravings.

531 MY REAL FRIEND, OR INCIDENTS IN LIFE, FOUNDED ON TRUTH. Second edition, corrected. *Darton*, 1812. A reprint of No. 530, with the same plates, but with a slightly different title and revised text.

532 LES ACCIDENS DE L'ENFANCE, PRÉSENTÉS DANS DE PETITES HISTORIETTES ... First edition, sm. 8vo. *A Paris, à la Librairie d'Education de Pierre Blanchard*, 1813. With an engraved frontispiece and title, and 8 charming half-page plates, all hand-coloured.

533 MAMMA'S STORIES, READ BY HERSELF TO HER LITTLE GIRL. First edition, sq. 12mo. *Darton*, 1814. With 8 full-page engravings, one shewing a doll's house, open and fully furnished.

534 JULIA AND FANNY, THE TWO FRIENDS ; OR, THE PLEASURES OF KINDNESS AND REWARD OF INDUSTRY . . . First edition, sq. 12mo. *Dean & Munday*, [*ca.* 1815]. With four coloured engravings'

535 LITTLE TRUTHS, FOR THE INSTRUCTION OF CHILDREN. VOL. I. First edition, sm. 8vo. *Darton*, 1816. Numerous copper engravings.

536 THE YELLOW SHOE STRINGS ; OR, THE GOOD EFFECTS OF OBEDIENCE TO PARENTS. First edition, sm. 8vo. *Darton*, 1816. With folding frontispiece and two other engravings.

537 DAME TRUELOVE'S TALES, NOW FIRST PUBLISHED AS USEFUL LESSONS FOR LITTLE MISSES AND MASTERS. First edition, sq. 12mo. *Harris*, [1817]. Engraved frontispiece and 22 engravings, all in colour.

538 DRAMAS FOR CHILDREN ; OR GENTLE REPROOFS FOR THEIR FAULTS. TRANSLATED FROM THE FRENCH OF L. F. JAUFFRET, BY THE EDITOR OF TABART'S POPULAR STORIES. First edition, 12mo. *Godwin*, 1817.

539 TALES FOR PLAY-HOURS ; OR, INTERESTING ANECDOTES, FOR THE AMUSEMENT AND IMPROVEMENT OF YOUTH. First edition, sm. 8vo. *Darton*, 1819.

540 HOW TO BE HAPPY : OR, THE COTTAGE OF CONTENT ; THE COTTAGE ON FIRE ; AND THE WATER-CRESS BAY. BY MRS. KANTISH. First edition, sm. 8vo. *Dean & Munday*, [*ca.* 1820]. With 13 coloured engravings.

541 THE REWARD OF MERIT : A NUMBER OF PICTURES, WITH SUITABLE STORIES, CIRCULATED TO AMUSE THE CURIOUS, AND INSTRUCT THE IGNORANT. First edition, 12mo. *Hodgson*, [*ca.* 1820]. With 4 coloured woodcuts.

543 THE SCHOOL OF INDUSTRY AND FRUGALITY ; OR, HIGHWAY TO THE TEMPLE OF HONOUR ... BEING BRIGHT EXAMPLES FOR ALL CHILDREN. First edition, 12mo. *Hodgson*, [*ca.* 1825]. With frontispiece, vignette title and 14 head-pieces, all in colour, mostly of trades.

544 EARLY IMPRESSIONS ; OR MORAL AND IN-STRUCTIVE ENTERTAINMENT FOR CHILDREN IN PROSE AND VERSE. First edition, sm. 8vo. *Hatchard*, 1828. With 12 illustrations by Dighton, early examples of lithography. Presentation copy from the author to the artist. A fine copy.

545 HISTORY OF ANN AND HER SEVEN SISTERS. First edition, 8vo. *Carvalho*, 1830. With 12 hand-coloured woodcuts.

SECTION V: CHRISTMAS BOOKS

546 A CHRISTMAS-BOX FOR MASTERS AND MISSES. First edition, 2 vols. in 1, 16mo. *Crowder*, *ca.* 1750. With 2 engraved titles and 5 engravings by T. Jefferys.

547 CHRISTMAS TALES FOR THE AMUSEMENT AND INSTRUCTION OF YOUNG LADIES AND GENTLE-MEN ... BY SOLOMON SOBERSIDES. First edition, 12mo. *Marshall*, [*ca.* 1785]. With frontispiece and 27 cuts.

548 CHRISTMAS TALES. 16mo. *Gainsborough* : *Mozley*, 1795. A piracy of No. 547, with different illustrations.

549 THE CHRISTMAS RIME OR, THE MUMMER'S OWN BOOK. BY LITTLE MASTER DOUBT WHO WITH HIS BROOM WILL SWEEP THEM OUT. ALSO, THE CHILDREN'S PRETTY RHIMES, OF SWING-SWANG, PEG TOP, ETC. 32mo. *Belfast* : *J. Smith*, [*ca.* 1806]. An extremely rare little book of an Irish version of the Christmas Mummers, with 12 woodcuts, one of each mummer, and six others to the nursery rhymes. The mummer's play opens with an introduction by Punchinello and the characters include St. George, the Turkey Champion, St. Patrick, Oliver Cromwell, and little Devil Doubt. Pages 4 and 5 are an alphabet.

550 THE LOST CHILD : A CHRISTMAS TALE. FOUNDED UPON A FACT. First edition, fcap. 8vo. *Harris*, 1810. With frontispiece and 4 charming engravings in colour.

551 THE TWELVE DAYS OF CHRISTMAS, SUNG AT PIPPIN'S HALL. First edition, 12mo. *Pitts*, [*ca.* 1810]. This is a round game with directions for playing, illustrated with numerous woodcuts.

552 CHRISTMAS TALES ; FOR THE AMUSEMENT AND INSTRUCTION OF YOUNG LADIES AND GENTLE-MEN IN WINTER EVENINGS. *Marshall, ca.* 1815.

553 THE PANTOMIME. *March, ca.* 1840. This Christmas entertainment is a version of the Harlequinade.

SECTION VI : STORIES ABOUT ANIMALS

(*a*) **Birds.**

554 [KENDALL (E. A.)]. THE CANARY BIRD : A MORAL FICTION INTERSPERSED WITH POETRY. First edition, 12mo. *E. Newbery*, 1799.

555 THE HISTORY OF A GOLDFINCH : ADDRESSED TO CHILDREN AS A REWARD FOR OBEDIENCE. First edition, 12mo. *Darton*, 1806. With two full-page hand-coloured engravings and one engraved vignette.

556 THE BLACKBIRD'S NEST ; A TALE FOR CHILDREN. First edition, 16mo. *Darton*, 1809. Engraved vignette on title and numerous other engravings.

557 THE HISTORY OF THE CELEBRATED NANNY GOOSE, FROM THE ORIGINAL MS. First edition, sm. 8vo. *For S. Hood*, 1813.

(*b*) **Cats and Dogs.**

558 [COVENTRY (F.)]. THE HISTORY OF POMPEY THE LITTLE ; OR, THE LIFE AND ADVENTURES OF A LAP-DOG. Second edition, sm. 8vo. *M. Cooper*, 1751. (See also No. 515).

559 MRS. PILKINGTON. MARVELLOUS ADVENTURES ; OR, THE VICISSITUDES OF A CAT. First edition, 12mo. *Vernor and Hood, etc.*, 1802.

560 [THE ADVENTURES OF A CAT, A DOG, AND A MONKEY. *ca.* 1805].

561 THE ADVENTURES OF LITTLE DOG TRIM AND HIS FUNNY COMPANIONS. First edition (?), 8vo. *G. Martin*, [*ca.* 1810]. With 16 hand-coloured engravings, and engraved text Also known with a different imprint, but with the same plates.

562 THE LITTLE WARBLER OF THE COTTAGE, AND HER DOG CONSTANT. First edition, 12mo. *Harris*, 1816. With six coloured engravings.

563 BIOGRAPHY OF A SPANIEL ... First edition, 12mo. *A. K. Newman & Co.*, 1826.

564 THE STORY OF LITTLE MARY AND HER CAT, IN WORDS NOT EXCEEDING TWO SYLLABLES. First edition, sm. 8vo. *Darton, ca.* 1835.

565 AUNT AFFABLE'S STORIES ABOUT DOGS. 8vo. *Dean & Co., ca.* 1840.

(c) Donkeys.

566 ARABELLA ANGUS. FURTHER ADVENTURES OF JENNY DONKEY ... First edition, 12mo. *Darton*, 1821.

(d) Hares.

567 THE HARE AND MANY FRIENDS, A FABULOUS TALE. Second edition, 12mo. *Orme*, 1810. With 8 engravings by W. Orme.

568 HARE AND MANY FRIENDS. 8vo. *For the Booksellers. ca.* 1850.

569 THE ESCAPES, WANDERINGS AND PRESERVATION OF A HARE. First edition, 12mo. *Evans, ca.* 1820. With 10 coloured woodcuts.

(e) Horses.

570 AUNT AFFABLE'S STORIES ABOUT HORSES. 8vo. *Dean & Co., ca.* 1850.

(f) Lambs.

571 and **572** THE PET LAMB, IN RHYTHM, INTENDED AS AN EXERCISE FOR THE MEMORY OF CHILDREN. TO WHICH IS ADDED, THE LADDER OF LEARNING AND THE ROBIN. BY J. B. First edition, sm. 8vo. *Darton*, [*ca.* 1825]. Two copies, one coloured and one uncoloured.

(g) Mice.

573 THE CURIOUS ADVENTURES OF A LITTLE WHITE MOUSE ; OR A BAD BOY CHANGED, IN A VERY COMICAL MANNER, INTO A GOOD BOY. First edition, 12mo. *Printed, and Sold by all the Booksellers in Town and Country,* [*ca.* 1780]. With frontispiece and numerous small cuts.

574 THE MICE, AND THEIR PIC-NIC. A GOOD MORAL TALE. BY A LOOKING-GLASS MAKER. 12mo. *Darton,* 1813. First published in 1810. Six full-page woodcuts.

575 LITTLE DOWNY ; OR, THE HISTORY OF A FIELD MOUSE. First edition, sm. 8vo. *Newman,* 1822. With coloured vignette title and 12 coloured engravings.

576 YOUNG NIBBLE, THE DISCONTENTED MOUSE. First edition, sm. sq. 8vo. *Dean,* [*ca.* 1825]. With 10 coloured engravings.

577 BEATRIX POTTER. THE TALE OF TWO BAD MICE. First edition, 12mo. 1904.

(h) Monkeys.

578 THE COMICAL ADVENTURES AT SEA AND ON SHORE OF JACKO THE BABOON. BY AN EYE-WITNESS. First edition, 8vo. *B. Blake, ca.* 1810.

579 THE MONKEY'S FROLIC. A HUMOROUS TALE. 8vo. *Harris, ca.* 1825.

(i) Squirrel.

580 THE LIFE OF BRUSHTAIL THE SQUIRREL, THAT COULD PLAY AND NOT QUARREL. First edition, sq. 12mo. *Aldis,* 1806. Engraved throughout, with 12 hand-coloured plates.

(k) Animals in General.

582 A POETICAL DESCRIPTION OF BEASTS, WITH MORAL REFLECTIONS FOR THE AMUSEMENT OF CHILDREN. First edition, 12mo. *Carnan,* 1773. With engraved frontispiece portrait of H.R.H. Prince William Henry, to whom the book is dedicated, and a woodcut of each of the 32 animals at the head of a poem about it.

583 A PRETTY BOOK OF PICTURES FOR LITTLE MASTERS AND MISSES : OR, TOMMY TRIP'S HISTORY OF BEASTS AND BIRDS . . . TO WHICH IS PREFIX'D THE HISTORY OF LITTLE TOM TRIP HIMSELF, OF HIS DOG JOULER, AND OF WOGGLOG THE GREAT GIANT . . . Twelfth edition, sq. 16mo. *Printed for the Booksellers* . . . [*ca.* 1785]. With frontispiece and numerous cuts in the text by Bewick.

"Tommy Trip" was one of Newbery's most successful inventions. Goldsmith refers to him in *The Vicar of Wakefield.*

584 THE NATURAL HISTORY OF FOUR FOOTED BEASTS. BY TOMMY TRIP. *Glasgow : Robertson,* 1791. With 48 charming cuts of animals.

585 STORIES OF ANIMALS, INTENDED FOR CHILDREN BETWEEN FIVE AND SEVEN YEARS OLD. 12mo. *Harvey and Darton,* 1831.

SECTION VII : **BOOKS ABOUT THE COUNTRYSIDE**

586 RURAL SCENES OR A PEEP INTO THE COUNTRY FOR CHILDREN. First edition, sm. 8vo. *Darton,* [1813].

587 THE PROGRESS OF THE DAIRY ; ILLUSTRATED WITH EIGHT ENGRAVINGS DESCRIPTIVE OF THE METHOD OF MAKING BUTTER AND CHEESE; FOR THE INFORMATION OF YOUTH. 12mo. *Wallis*, 1815.

588 W. (S.). A VISIT TO A FARM HOUSE ... Seventh edition, revised and corrected by T. A. *Darton*, 1820.

589 A VISIT TO GROVE COTTAGE FOR THE ENTERTAINMENT AND INSTRUCTION OF CHILDREN. First edition, sm. 8vo. *Harris*, 1823. With coloured, engraved title and numerous coloured engravings.

590 THE FARM YARD QUADRILLE. First edition, sq. 12mo. *Uxbridge*: *Printed by William Lake, etc.*, 1825. With four charming plates in colour.

591 ELLIOTT (MARY). RUSTIC EXCURSIONS TO AID TARRY-AT-HOME TRAVELLERS ... CONTINUATION OF RUSTIC EXCURSIONS. First edition, 2 vols. in 1, sm. 8vo. *Darton*, [1825]. With 48 half-page coloured engravings.

592 [THE SEASONS. *ca.* 1825]. A series of 12 charming coloured engravings of the months of the year, shewing the recreations of youth, below each a short verse.

593 TAYLOR (J.). THE FARM ; A NEW ACCOUNT OF RURAL TOILS AND PRODUCE. First edition, sq. 12mo. *Harris*, 1832. With 8 engravings on steel and 26 on wood.

594 COUNTRY SCENES, OR THE KIND GRANDFATHER. First edition, fcap. 8vo. *Lacey*, [*ca.* 1835]. With 12 half-page coloured woodcuts.

595 EMMA'S VISIT TO THE COUNTRY. Cr. 8vo. *Belper*: *Rosewarne, ca.* 1840.

595a MY UNCLE'S FARM. *Liverpool : Philip, Son & Nephew, ca.* 1865. A double jig-saw, with a map of Europe on the reverse side.

SECTION VIII: BOOKS FOR CHILDREN BY AUTHORS FAMOUS IN OTHER SPHERES

JOHN BUNYAN

596 DIVINE EMBLEMS : OR TEMPORAL THINGS SPIRITUALIZED. FITTED FOR THE USE OF BOYS AND GIRLS. 12mo. *Coventry : Luckman, etc.,* [*ca.* 1775].

596a SCENES FROM THE PILGRIM'S PROGRESS BY JOHN BUNYAN. *B. Blake, ca.* 1805. Twelve full-page coloured engravings from the story with the figures in early nineteenth century clothes.

597 BUNYAN EXPLAINED TO A CHILD ; BEING PICTURES AND POEMS, FOUNDED UPON THE PILGRIM'S PROGRESS . . . BY THE REV. ISAAC TAYLOR, ONGAR. First edition, 8vo. *F. Westley,* 1824.

598 BUNYANO (DON STEPHANO). THE PRETTIEST BOOK FOR CHILDREN ; BEING THE HISTORY OF THE ENCHANTED CASTLE ; SITUATED IN ONE OF THE FORTUNATE ISLES . . . First edition, 12mo. *F. Newbery,* 1772. Extremely rare. Not in Welsh. A very odd farrago, with a remote relation to Bunyan's story, interspersed with lessons and concluding with an educational dialogue by " Giant Instruction." With frontispiece " portrait of the author," and numerous small cuts.

599 EXPLANATION OF THE PILGRIM'S PROGRESS . . . ABRIDGED AND ADAPTED TO THE CAPACITIES OF CHILDREN, IN DIALOGUE BETWEEN A CHILD AND HIS MOTHER. BY A LADY. First edition, sm. sq. 8vo. *J. Barfield*, 1808. With seven full-page engravings.

SAMUEL BUTLER

600 HUDIBRAS. *ca.* 1840. A card game based on incidents from the famous sixteenth century satire.

WILLIAM COWPER

601 A SECOND HOLIDAY FOR JOHN GILPIN ; OR A VOYAGE TO VAUXHALL . . . First edition, sq. 12mo. *Wallis*, 1808. With folding panoramic frontispiece of Vauxhall Gardens and four full-page engravings, all in colour. A " sequel " not by Cowper.

601a THE DIVERTING HISTORY OF JOHN GILPIN . . . WITH SIX ILLUSTRATIONS BY GEORGE CRUIKSHANK . . . First edition, 12mo. *Tilt*, 1828.

602 JOHN GILPIN'S DIVERTING RIDE TO EDMONTON. ILLUSTRATED BY [PERCY] CRUIKSHANK. *Read & Co., ca.* 1845.

603 AUNT LOUISA'S LONDON TOY BOOKS. JOHN GILPIN. *Warne, ca.* 1865.

604 THE DIVERTING HISTORY OF JOHN GILPIN . . . WRITTEN BY WM. COWPER. WITH DRAWINGS BY R. CALDECOTT. *Routledge, ca.* 1880.

DANIEL DEFOE AND HIS IMITATORS

605 THE WODNERFUL (*sic*) LIFE, AND MOST SUR-PRIZING ADVENTURES OF ROBINSON CRUSOE, OF YORK ; MARINER . . . Sm. 8vo. *Hitch*, *etc.*, 1741. An extremely scarce and early chapbook edition. In three parts ; with numerous cuts. These early chapbooks are the first adaptation of the story for children.

606 THE WONDERFUL LIFE ... OF ROBINSON CRUSOE ... FAITHFULLY EPITOMIZED ... 12mo. *For Edw. Midwinter*, [*ca.* 1750]. A rare chapbook edition with cuts.

607 THE WONDERFUL LIFE AND MOST SURPRISING ADVENTURES OF ROBINSON CRUSOE OF YORK, MARINER ... FAITHFULLY EPITOMIZED. Sm. 8vo. *Glasgow : Printed for the Booksellers*, 1784. A rare chapbook edition, with numerous cuts.

608 THE WONDERFUL LIFE ... OF ROBINSON CRUSOE ... 12mo. *R. Carpue & D. Capua*, *ca.* 1790.

609 THE WONDERFUL LIFE ... OF ROBINSON CRUSOE. 12mo. *Darton*, 1809. With 8 full-page cuts. The woodcut on the front wrapper shows a balloon in the air.

610 THE WONDERFUL LIFE ... OF ROBINSON CRUSOE ... Sm. 8vo. *Darton*, 1815.

611 THE WONDERFUL LIFE AND SURPRISING ADVENTURES OF THAT RENOWNED HERO, ROBINSON CRUSOE ... Sq. 16mo. *Darton*, 1815.

612 THE LIFE AND ADVENTURES OF ROBINSON CRUSOE, OF YORK, MARINER, WRITTEN BY HIMSELF. *York : J. Kendrew*, *ca.* 1820. Chapbook versions of the story were especially popular in York, Crusoe's reputed birthplace.

613 THE WONDERFUL LIFE ... OF ROBINSON CRUSOE ... 12mo. *Darton*, 1826. With folding frontispiece and 3 plates, all engraved.

614 THE NEW ROBINSON CRUSOE ; AN INSTRUC-
TIVE AND ENTERTAINING HISTORY. Sm. 8vo.
Dublin : Smith, 1827. A very free chapbook
adaptation. Woodcuts.

615 BYSH'S EDITION OF THE LIFE OF ROBINSON
CRUSOE ... 12mo. *J. Bysh, ca.* 1840.
With 8 coloured cuts.

616 ROBINSON CRUSOE ... *For the Booksellers,
ca.* 1845.

616a POOR ROBINSON. *ca.* 1840. An ingenious
perspective toy-book, possibly of French
origin.

617 THE HERMIT : OR, THE UNPARALLELED
SUFFERINGS AND SURPRISING ADVENTURES OF
PHILIP QUARLL, AN ENGLISHMAN : WHO WAS
LATELY DISCOVERED UPON AN UNINHABITED
ISLAND IN THE SOUTH SEA ; WHERE HE LIVED
ABOUT FIFTY YEARS ... A New Edition, with
an elegant frontispiece, 8vo. *For William
Lane at the Minerva Press,* 1794. The
original Minerva Press edition was in 1786.

618 PHILIP QUARLL, THE ENGLISH HERMIT, OR
THE ADVENTURES OF, ... 12mo. *Gainsborough
Mozley,* 1807.

619 J. H. CAMPE. ROBINSON DER JÜNGERE, ZUR
ANGENEHMEN UND NÜTZLICHEN UNTERHAL-
TUNG FÜR KINDER. First edition, 2 vols.,
contemporary crimson German morocco,
with a rococo design tooled in gilt (a different
design on each volume), pale blue silk end-
leaves, one in each volume stamped in gilt
with the name of the original owner and the
dates, 1779, 1780, all within a diamond-
shaped floral gilt frame, gilt gauffred edges,
sm. 8vo. *Hamburg beim Verfasser und in
Commission bei Carl Ernst Bohn,* 1779-1780.
Campe appears to have been among the first

121

to grasp the possibilities of the Robinson Crusoe story as entertainment and, be it said, as instruction for the young. In his long preface, in which he refers to Defoe's character as the " Old " Robinson and to his own as the " New," he explains how he grafted Rousseau's natural savage on to Defoe's castaway. Campe himself translated his story into French (1779), and English (1781), but the English version that achieved wide popularity was one published by Stockdale in 1788, and illustrated by John Bewick (see No. 620). The original German edition is as rare as any child's book in any language. It is in the same class, for rarity, as the " Alice " of 1865. Such a handsome copy, in such fine condition, is of course, especially desirable and we venture to doubt whether its equal could be found.

620 THE NEW ROBINSON CRUSOE ; AN INSTRUC-TIVE AND ENTERTAINING HISTORY FOR THE USE OF CHILDREN OF BOTH SEXES. Translated from the French. First edition of this translation, 4 vols. in 2, 12mo. *Stockdale*, 1788. Extremely rare. On the title-page of the fourth volume only, is the note " Price 6s. sewed in four volumes, or 7s. bound in two," which leads us to presume that the four-volume edition is slightly anterior to that in two volumes. Campe himself trans-lated the book into English and published it at Hamburg in 1781, but, as Darton remarks, the edition that popularized the story in England was this one of 1788. The thirty-two full-page cuts are by John Bewick, some of them are signed by him. Hugo (33) quotes only the 2-vol. edition. It is one of the rarest books illustrated by John Bewick.

621 THE NEW ROBINSON CRUSOE, DESIGNED FOR THE AMUSEMENT AND INSTRUCTION OF THE YOUTH OF BOTH SEXES. Translated from the original German. 16mo. *E. Newbery*, 1790.

622 [J. D. R. WYSS]. LE ROBINSON SUISSE, OU JOURNAL D'UN PÈRE DE FAMILLE NAUFRAGÉ AVEC SES ENFANS. TRADUIT DE L'ALLEMAND DE M. WISS ; PAR MME. DE MONTOLIEU . . . *A Paris, Chez Arthus Bertrand* . . . 1814. First edition of the translation. Wyss's *Der Schweizerische Robinson* was originally published at Zürich in two parts, in 1812-13. Madame de Montholieu found the ending of the original too abrupt and, with the author's permission, altered and considerably enlarged it, greatly improving the story in the process. Her principal addition was the figure of the donkey. She offered the use of her version to Wyss, but he was already slightly ashamed of indentifying himself with a story for children and therefore declined.

623 THE FAMILY ROBINSON CRUSOE : OR, JOURNAL OF A FATHER SHIPWRECKED, WITH HIS WIFE AND CHILDREN, ON AN UNINHABITED ISLAND. TRANSLATED FROM THE GERMAN OF M. WISS. *M. J. Godwin and Co.*, 1816. This is the first translation into English of *The Swiss Family Robinson*, but not the first edition of it, which appeared in 1814. For some unexplained reason it consists of the first part only. The bibliography of the English editions would repay investigation. It was probably W. H. G. Kingston, in 1849, who coined the title by which the story is now known in England, and he was also responsible for giving it its present form.

624 EDGEWORTH (MARIA). MORAL TALES FOR YOUNG PEOPLE. First edition, 5 vols. in 3, sm. 8vo. A typical example of Miss Edgeworth's numerous writings for children. Her father, in the preface, describes these tales for young people of an advanced age as intended neither to " dissipate the attention, nor inflame the imagination." Alas, Miss Edgeworth, like so many other writers of " moral tales," was insufficiently aware that, in Scott's words, " The rats won't go into the trap if they smell the rat-catcher." (*Cf.* Slade, *Maria Edgeworth*, Constable, 1937).

625 [SARAH FIELDING]. THE GOVERNESS ; OR, THE LITTLE FEMALE ACADEMY. CALCULATED FOR THE ENTERTAINMENT AND INSTRUCTION OF YOUNG LADIES IN THEIR EDUCATION. Fifth edition, sm. 8vo. *For A. Millar*, 1768. One of the earliest of " moral tales," by the sister of Henry Fielding. Its popularity was considerable and long-lasting. Mrs. Sherwood almost entirely rewrote the book because she disapproved of its two fairy-tales, although she " admitted " one of them. Mrs. Trimmer criticised the book severely on similar grounds.

626 [WILLIAM GODWIN]. FABLES ANCIENT AND MODERN. ADAPTED FOR THE USE OF CHILDREN FROM THREE TO EIGHT YEARS OF AGE. BY EDWARD BALDWIN, ESQ. First edition, 2 vols., sm. 8vo. *Hodgkins*, 1805. There is a tradition that the plates are by Blake and the preface by Lamb.

627 THE LOOKING-GLASS, A TRUE HISTORY OF THE EARLY YEARS OF AN ARTIST ; CALCULATED TO AWAKEN THE EMULATION OF YOUNG PERSONS

BY THEOPHILUS MARCLIFFE. First edition, 12mo. *Hodgkins*, 1805. With five copperplates. A biographical account of Mulready, illustrator of *The Peacock "at Home"* and designer of the Mulready envelope. With Godwin's 12 pp. catalogue of children's books.

628 LIFE OF LADY JANE GREY, AND OF LORD GUILDFORD HER HUSBAND . . . BY THEOPHILUS MARCLIFFE. First edition, 12mo. *Hodgkins*, 1806.

OLIVER GOLDSMITH.

629 THE HISTORY OF LITTLE GOODY TWO-SHOES; OTHERWISE CALLED MRS. MARGERY TWO-SHOES . . . . *J. Newbery*, 1766. This is one of the most interesting books in the exhibition, for it represents a major bibliographical discovery. This copy has been twice sold by auction as "the third edition." It is, in fact, the only known copy of the second edition, and, as no copy of the first edition is known to survive, and as this is the first record of the survival of a copy of the second edition, a short account of the evidence may be welcome.

The B.M. copy bears the words "Third Edition" on its title-page, and so does Ernest Hartley Coleridge's copy (Victoria and Albert Museum), from which Charles Welsh's fac-simile reprint was made in 1882. The fourth edition was dated 1767 (see Gumuchian Catalogue, No. 2753) and the fifth edition, 1768 (Bodleian Library). The book was originally published in 1765, but no copy of the first edition is known to have survived. The only possible explanation of the words "New Edition" on the title-page of the present copy, therefore, appears to be that

it is the second edition.   It is thus not only
the earliest edition now known, but it is also
unique.

The tradition associating Goldsmith's
name with the book is too strong to be ignored
but, whether he wrote it, or part of it,
whether he revised the text, or wrote only
the Introduction, as Charles Welsh wrote in
the Preface to his facsimile reprint, it still
remained true, sixty years later, that " few
nursery books have had a wider circulation,
or have retained their position so long."
The number of editions listed here is, in itself,
considerable evidence of that fact.

630 THE HISTORY OF LITTLE GOODY TWO-SHOES
... *J. Newbery*, 1766.   Charles Welsh's
facsimile of the third edition.

632 THE HISTORY OF LITTLE GOODY TWO-SHOES
... 24mo.   *Printed for the Proprietors, and
sold by all the Booksellers in Town and Country*
[176—].   An extremely interesting early
pirated edition.   It has different cuts from
the Newbery edition ; although they are
copied from those, the figures and back-
grounds are quite different.

633 THE HISTORY OF LITTLE GOODY TWO-SHOES
... 24mo.   *T. Carnan and F. Newbery*, 1770.

633a THE HISTORY OF LITTLE GOODY TWO-SHOES
... The First Worcester edition.   *Printed at
Worcester, Massachusetts, By Isaiah Thomas*
... 1787.   The rare first American edition,
in its original binding.   The cuts are quite
different from those in Newbery's edition,
although based on them.

634 THE HISTORY OF LITTLE GOODY TWO-SHOES ... *Printed for the Booksellers*, [178—]. Also an interesting early edition with cuts adapted by another hand from Newbery's. Despite the London imprint on the title-page, this has at the end a 2½-page list of books sold by Hall & Elliot, Newcastle, including many Newbery titles.

635 THE HISTORY OF LITTLE GOODY TWO-SHOES ... 24mo. *Carnan*, 1783. The frontispiece is in facsimile.

636 THE HISTORY OF GOODY TWO SHOES .. *Darton*, 1793. Possibly the earliest edition published by Darton. With engraved title and frontispiece and adaptations of the Newbery cuts.

637 THE HISTORY OF LITTLE GOODY TWO-SHOES ... 12mo. *York: Wilson and Spence*, 1803. With a new series of cuts.

638 THE HISTORY OF LITTLE GOODY TWO-SHOES. 12mo. *Burslem: J. Tregortha*, 1802. With a miniature child's bookplate on pink paper: "Mary Hutton Reynolds." A new series of cuts.

639 THE MODERN GOODY TWO-SHOES ... BY MARY BELSON. First edition, sm. 8vo. *Darton*, 1819. With folding frontispiece and two other engravings. *Darton*, 1819.

640 GOODY TWO SHOES ; EXEMPLIFYING THE GOOD CONSEQUENCES OF EARLY ATTENTION TO LEARNING AND VIRTUE. Sm. 8vo. *Darton*, [1819]. A reprint of No. 639, undated, and without the author's name.

641 THE HISTORY OF GOODY TWO-SHOES, WITH THE ADVENTURES OF HER BROTHER TOMMY. 12mo. *Glasgow: Lumsden*, [ca. 1820]. A very freely adapted version of the original.

642 GOODY TWO SHOES ; OR, THE HISTORY OF LITTLE MARGERY MEANWELL, IN RHYME. Sq. 12mo. *Harris*, 1825. The wrapper is dated 1833. With 20 engraved head-pieces.

643 THE ORPHAN ; OR THE ENTERTAINING HISTORY OF LITTLE GOODY GOOSECAP. CONTAINING A VARIETY OF ADVENTURES CALCULATED TO AMUSE AND INSTRUCT THE LILLIPUTIAN WORLD. BY TOBY TEACHEM. First edition, 12mo. *Marshall, ca.* 1780. A very rare and quite barefaced copy of the original, the incidents of which it follows fairly closely.

644 THE ENTERTAINING HISTORY OF LITTLE GOODY GOOSECAP, CONTAINING A VARIETY OF ADVENTURES CALCULATED TO AMUSE AND INSTRUCT THE LILLIPUTIAN WORLD. *Marshall, ca.* 1790. The double address on the title-page betrays the fact that this is a reprint. Apart from the frontispiece all the cuts are the same. With engraved title and frontispiece. Woodcuts in the text.

644a LITTLE GOODY GOOSECAP ... 8vo. *Harris,* 1818.

645 THE RENOWNED HISTORY OR PRIMROSE PRETTYFACE, WHO, BY HER SWEETNESS OF TEMPER, AND LOVE OF LEARNING, WAS RAISED FROM BEING THE DAUGHTER OF A POOR COTTAGER, TO GREAT RICHES, AND THE DIGNITY OF LADY OF THE MANOR ... First edition, 12mo. *Marshall,* [*ca.* 1790]. This also follows the detail of the original closely.

646 A COLLECTION OF THE MOST APPROVED ENTERTAINING STORIES CALCULATED FOR THE INSTRUCTION AND AMUSEMENT OF ALL THE MASTERS AND MISSES OF THIS VAST EMPIRE. BY SOLOMON WINLOVE, ESQ. The Second Edition, revised and corrected. *For F.*

Newbery, 1770. The grounds for attributing the editorship of this volume to Goldsmith are extremely slender. The stories include " Jack Horner," " Cinderella," and " Red Riding Hood." The earliest mention of the book known to Welsh is in E. Newbery's list for 1789.

647 A COLLECTION OF THE MOST APPROVED ENTERTAINING STORIES. BY SOLOMON WIN-LOVE. A New Edition. *E. Newbery,* [*ca.* 1780].

648 THE TWELFTH-DAY GIFT ; OR, THE GRAND EXHIBITION . . . First edition, 16mo. *J. Newbery,* 1767. A very fine copy of this extremely rare book.
" Dedicated to the Duke of Galaxy, Marquis of Setstar, the Countess of Twilight . . ." Welsh describes only an imperfect fourth edition of 1776. The British Museum has a copy published by Carnan, 1783.

649 GOLDSMITH'S ELEGY ON THE DEATH OF A MAD DOG. First juvenile edition, sm. 8vo. *Hodgson, ca.* 1810.

650 AN ELEGY ON THE DEATH OF A MAD DOG, WRITTEN BY DR. GOLDSMITH, PICTURED BY R. CALDECOTT, SUNG BY MASTER BILL PRIMROSE. *Routledge, ca.* 1880. First edition illustrated by Caldecott.

651 DR. GOLDSMITH'S CELEBRATED ELEGY, ON THAT GLORY OF HER SEX, MRS. MARY BLAIZE. First juvenile edition, sq. 16mo. *Harris,* 1808. A fine copy, engraved throughout, title, text and plates.

652 AN ELEGY ON THE GLORY OF HER SEX, MRS. MARY BLAIZE. BY DR. OLIVER GOLDSMITH. *Routledge, ca.* 1880. First edition, illustrated by Caldecott.

653 THE DRAWING SCHOOL FOR LITTLE MASTERS AND MISSES : CONTAINING THE MOST EASY AND CONCISE RULES FOR LEARNING TO DRAW, WITHOUT THE ASSISTANCE OF A TEACHER. EMBELLISHED WITH A GREAT VARIETY OF FIGURES CURIOUSLY DESIGNED. TO WHICH ARE ADDED, THE WHOLE ART OF KITE MAKING; AND THE AUTHOR'S NEW DISCOVERIES IN THE PREPARATION OF WATER COLOURS. BY MASTER MICHAEL ANGELO. First edition, 12mo. *Carnan*, 1773. Exceedingly rare. Gumuchian's earliest edition was 1777. Welsh, p. 207, says it was entered at Stationers' Hall by Carnan, 4th Jan., 1773, but the earliest edition he quotes is 1774. A fine copy, with engraved title and frontispiece, and numerous cuts in the text.

654 THE NEWTONIAN SYSTEM OF PHILOSOPHY ADAPTED TO THE CAPACITIES OF YOUNG GENTLEMEN AND LADIES ... BY TOM TELESCOPE. Fifth edition, 16mo. *Carnan and Newbery*, 1779. Extremely scarce. The earliest edition described by Welsh, who thinks it " not at all unlikely that this book was written by O. Goldsmith," is the seventh, dated 1787.

With full-page engravings, possibly by Stothard and Blake. At the end is a list of 64 publications of Carnan and Newbery.

CHARLES LAMB.

655 BEAUTY AND THE BEAST. Second edition, full crimson morocco, original wrapper with imprint of M. I. Godwin bound in, edges gilt on the rough, sq. 12mo. *Jackson*, 1825. With 8 coloured plates and the folding sheet of music. This edition appears to be unrecorded. Its sub-title is " The Enchanted Rose." Although the imprint on the title is that of

William Jackson, the original wrappers are Godwin's. The text is the " surprise " edition and the book appears to consist of first edition sheets with a new title. This is borne out by the watermark, whichis 1810.

656 THE KING AND QUEEN OF HEARTS ; WITH THE ROGUERIES OF THE KNAVE WHO STOLE THE QUEEN'S PIES. First edition, 12mo. *Godwin*, 1809. Engraved throughout with coloured title and 14 coloured engravings. The wrappers and 3 leaves of the text are from the facsimile reprint.

657 KING AND QUEEN OF SPADES AND KING AND QUEEN OF CLUBS. [*ca.* 1807]. Twenty-eight coloured engravings, no wrappers, but the text complete.

658 TALES FROM SHAKESPEARE, DESIGNED FOR THE USE OF YOUNG PERSONS. Second edition, 2 vols., sm. 8vo. *Godwin*, 1810. Exceedingly rare. The first edition was published in 1807. This edition has the 20 engravings.

659 [ALAIN RENÉ LE SAGE]. THE ADVENTURES OF GIL BLAS OF SANTILLANE, ABRIDGED. *E. Newbery*, 1788. Extremely rare ; this juvenile version of " Gil Blas " is not recorded by Welsh in any edition. Several full-page woodcuts.

660 [THOMAS LOVE PEACOCK]. SIR HORNBOOK ; OR CHILDE LANCELOT'S EXPEDITION. First edition, 12mo. *Sharpe and Hailes*, 1814.

661 SIR HORNBOOK . . . Second edition, sq. 12mo. *Sharpe*, 1815. A coloured copy.

662 THE HOME TREASURY. THE FAVORITE BALLADS OF CHEVY CHASE AND SIR HORNBOOK . . . EDITED BY FELIX SUMMERLY. *Chapman and Hall*, ca. 1880.

663 [SAMUEL RICHARDSON]. THE HISTORY OF SIR CHARLES GRANDISON, ABRIDGED FROM THE WORKS OF SAMUEL RICHARDSON, ESQ. . . . 12mo. *E. Newbery*, 1789. 12mo. The earliest edition given by Welsh, p. 300, which he quotes from a list only. Gumuchian, however, No. 4752, has an edition of 1783. Engraved frontispiece and 4 engravings.

664 [TOBIAS SMOLLETT]. THE COMICAL ADVENTURES OF RODERICK RANDOM, AND HIS FRIEND STRAP, WITH THEIR VOYAGE TO SOUTH AMERICA, ETC. First edition, sq. 16mo. *Brentford: P. Norbury*, [*ca.* 1785]. Extremely rare. With a frontispiece and cuts in the text.

665 [ROBERT SOUTHEY]. THE STORY OF THE THREE BEARS. *Porter and Wright*, 1837. First published in the four volumes of *The Doctor* ; this appears to be the first separate edition. There is a dedicatory poem to "The Unknown Author of ' The Doctor.' " Illustrated.

666 [AGNES STRICKLAND]. THE MOSS-HOUSE : IN WHICH MANY OF THE WORKS OF NATURE ARE RENDERED A SOURCE OF AMUSEMENT TO CHILDREN. First edition, 12mo. *Darton*, 1822. (See also No. 677).

667 [JONATHAN SWIFT]. TRAVELS INTO SEVERAL REMOTE NATIONS OF THE WORLD. IN FOUR PARTS. BY LEMUEL GULLIVER, FIRST A SURGEON, AND THEN A CAPTAIN OF SEVERAL SHIPS. Two vols. in one, 8vo. *Printed by Benj. Motte* . . . 1726. This is what is sometimes called the second issue of the first edition. In fact, as Harold Williams has shewn (*Library*, 4th ser., Vol. VI, 1926, pp. 229-263) it is the second edition.

668 GULLIVER'S VOYAGE TO LILLIPUT . . . *For the Booksellers*, 1816.

669 MARY WOLLSTONECRAFT. ORIGINAL STORIES FROM REAL LIFE ; WITH CONVERSATIONS, CALCULATED TO REGULATE THE AFFECTIONS, AND FORM THE MIND TO TRUTH AND GOODNESS. First edition, 12mo. *Johnson*, 1791. The frontispiece and the five other engraved plates are by Blake.

SECTION IX : BOOKS OF TRADES

670 LITTLE JACK OF ALL TRADES, WITH SUITABLE REPRESENTATIONS. First edition, 2 vols., sm. 8vo. *Darton & Harvey & Harris*, 1804-5. Extremely scarce. Tuer has an edition of 1810. Gumuchian 3819 (called " First Edition ") has the edition of 1823. Vol. I has a vignette title and 22 engravings including two of a printing press at work and one of a bookbinder, all in colour. Vol. II has vignette title and 22 engravings, including an auction sale of a picture by Loutherbourg, a paper-mill, etc.

671 LITTLE JACK OF ALL TRADES ; OR MECHANICAL ARTS DESCRIBED, IN PROSE AND VERSE. *Darton*, 1823. With 45 charming coloured engravings (3 to a page) of craftsmen at work. A re-issue, with new illustrations, of No. 670.

672 THE BOOK OF TRADES, OR LIBRARY OF THE USEFUL ARTS. 3 vols., 12mo. *Tabart*, 1806-5. With 67 engravings of trades and handicrafts. Vols. I and II third, Vol. III first edition.

673 THE PROGRESS OF THE QUARTERN LOAF. First edition, sq. 12mo. *N.P. or D.* [*ca.* 1810]. Engraved throughout, a series of six coloured plates, each with verses, shewing the making of bread.

674 A VISIT TO THE BAZAAR . . . First edition, 12mo. *Harris*, 1818. With 32 coloured engravings of the various departments of the Bazaar.

675 THE WHOLE HISTORY, IN VERSE, OF THAT WELL-KNOWN AND WELCOME GUEST, A GOOD PLUM PUDDING, FOR BOYS AND GIRLS. . . . First edition, sq. 12mo. *Darton*, 1814. With 32 half-page engravings of everything concerned with the making of a plum-pudding.

676 THE PROMISED VISIT : INCLUDING AN ACCOUNT OF THE VARIOUS METHODS OF MANUFACTUR-ING PAPER IN DIFFERENT COUNTRIES . . . First edition, 12mo. *Darton*, 1818. With engraved frontispiece.

677 THE LITTLE TRADESMAN ; OR, A PEEP INTO ENGLISH INDUSTRY. First edition, 8vo. *Darton, ca.*, 1825. With 24 engravings of trades and handicrafts. Bookplate of the Duke of Leeds. The author appears to have been Agnes Strickland. (See also No. 666).

678 CUFFY, THE NEGRO'S DOGGEREL DESCRIPTION OF THE PROGRESS OF SUGAR. *E. Wallis, ca.* 1825. With 15 full-page coloured cuts.

SECTION X: LONDON CRIES AND OTHER BOOKS ABOUT LONDON

679 THE CRIES OF LONDON AS THEY ARE DAILY EXHIBITED IN THE STREETS, WITH AN EPIGRAM IN VERSE ADAPTED TO EACH. TO WHICH IS ADDED, A DESCRIPTION OF THE METROPOLIS IN VERSE. First edition, 16mo. *E. Newbery*, 1784. Extremely rare. Welsh, p. 196, cites a copy from Newbery's list of 1789 and mentions that the Bodleian copy is dated 1704 (misprint for 1804). Our copy has a frontispiece and 58 full-page woodcuts of London Cries. Newbery's 6-page catalogue at the end. This appears to be the only recorded copy of the first edition of this book.

680 THE UNIVERSAL MEDLEY AND BOOK OF PICTURES ; CALCULATED TO AMUSE AND INSTRUCT LITTLE CHILDREN. First edition, sq. 16mo. *Darton, ca.* 1795. With 73 cuts of London Cries, children's toys, birds, beasts, etc. A charming book.

681 THE CRIES OF LONDON, DISPLAYING THE MANNERS, CUSTOMS, AND CHARACTERS, OF VARIOUS PEOPLE WHO TRAVERSE LONDON STREETS WITH ARTICLES TO SELL, TO WHICH IS ADDED SOME PRETTY POETRY APPLICABLE TO EACH CHARACTER, INTENDED TO AMUSE AND INSTRUCT ALL GOOD CHILDREN . . . BY TIMOTHY TICKLECHEEK. First edition, 12mo., *Fairburn,* 1797. With frontispiece, title, and 12 full-page plates, all engraved.

682 THE CRIES OF YORK. (IN TWO PARTS). FOR THE AMUSEMENT OF YOUNG CHILDREN. PART I. First edition, sq. 16mo. *York : Kendrew, ca.* 1800. With frontispiece and 12 cuts.

683 THE NEW CRIES OF LONDON, WITH CHARACTERISTIC ENGRAVINGS. First edition, sm. 8vo. *Darton,* 1804. With engraved vignette title and 22 engravings of London cries.

684 THE CRIES OF LONDON, AS THEY ARE EXHIBITED IN THE STREETS ; WITH AN EPIGRAM IN VERSE, ADAPTED TO EACH . . . TO WHICH IS PREFIXED, A POETICAL DESCRIPTION OF THE METROPOLIS. First edition, 12mo. *Harris,* 1804. The frontispiece shews Harris's shop, formerly Newbery's.

685 THE MOVING MARKET; OR CRIES OF LONDON : FOR THE AMUSEMENT AND INSTRUCTION OF GOOD CHILDREN. First edition, 24mo. *Wellington : Houlston, ca.* 1810.

686 THE CRIES OF LONDON, FOR THE INSTRUCTION AND AMUSEMENT OF GOOD CHILDREN. 24mo. *York : Killigrew,* [*ca.* 1810]. With 26 woodcuts.

687 LONDON MELODIES; OR, CRIES OF THE SEASONS. First edition, two parts in one vol., sm. 8vo. *Darton,* [1812]. Extremely scarce. With two vignette titles and 36 woodcuts of London Cries.

688 ROBIN GOODFELLOW. THE HISTORY OF GOG AND MAGOG, THE CHAMPIONS OF LONDON ... First edition, sm. 8vo. *Souter,* 1819. Three copper engravings.

689 THE MERRY CRIES AND SPORTS OF LONDON ... 24mo. *Whitrow,* [*ca.* 1820]. With 31 cuts of London cries and scenes.

690 NEW CRIES OF LONDON. BY J. BISHOP. First edition, 12mo. *Dean and Munday,* [*ca.* 1820], With pinprick frontispiece of St. Paul's, vignette title and 14 woodcuts, all coloured.

691 THE CRIES OF LONDON : DRAWN FROM LIFE, WITH DESCRIPTIVE LETTER-PRESS, IN VERSE AND PROSE. First edition, sm. 8vo. *Artists' Depository,* 1823. With engraved title and 23 full-page engravings, all in colour.

692a THE NEW CRIES OF LONDON ; OR, ITINERANT TRADES OF THE BRITISH METROPOLIS ... *Darton,* 1823.

692b THE CRIES OF LONDON. *Darton, ca.* 1825. Despite its four missing pieces the exceeding interest of this jig-saw puzzle has caused its inclusion here.

692c SAM SYNTAX'S DESCRIPTION OF THE CRIES OF LONDON ... Sm. 8vo. *Harris*, 1821. With 17 coloured woodcuts. The frontispiece shows St. Paul's Cathedral with the exterior of Harris's shop in the foreground.

693 LONDON SCENES; IN EASY LESSONS FOR CHILDREN. First edition, sm. 8vo. *Darton*, 1837. With 8 coloured woodcuts of scenes in London, including "The New Cab"—a Hansom; the mail-coach leaving the G.P.O.; an omnibus at the Bank of England; a Steamboat at London Bridge; a fire-engine; and a balloon.

694 PETER PARLEY'S VISIT TO LONDON, DURING THE CORONATION OF QUEEN VICTORIA. First edition, sq. 12mo. *Tilt*, 1839. Six plates of scenes from the Coronation.

695 WILLIAM AND LUCY'S TRIP TO LONDON. 8vo. *Park, ca.* 1840.

696 MARCH'S NEW 1D. CRIES OF LONDON. Sm. 8vo. *ca.* 1850. With coloured frontispiece and 18 cuts of London Cries.

697 CRIES OF LONDON. *T. Goode, ca.* 1850. Crude woodcuts, crudely coloured, in panorama form.

698 LONDON CRIES. ILLUSTRATED. FOR THE YOUNG. *Darton, ca.* 1860. The plates were originally used by Charles Tilt in 1833.

699 THE MODERN CRIES OF LONDON. ILLUSTRATED BY [PERCY] CRUIKSHANK. *Read & Co., ca.* 1865.

PART IV

Illustrated Books

SECTION I: **FAMOUS ILLUSTRATORS**

THE BEWICKS.

700 THE MIRROR ; OR, A LOOKING-GLASS FOR
YOUNG PEOPLE OF BOTH SEXES ; TO
MAKE THEM WISE, GOOD, AND HAPPY.
CONSISTING OF A CHOICE COLLECTION OF
FAIRY TALES. BY MOTHER GOOSE. *Newcastle
upon Tyne : Printed by T. Saint, for W.
Charnley, etc.,* 1778. This extraordinarily
interesting little volume seems to be unrecorded. Its 13 exquisite woodcut head-
pieces are undoubtedly the work of Bewick.
It includes one fairy-tale by Perrault—
Beauty and the Beast—and is the earliest
use we have found of the " Looking-Glass "
title, afterwards so consistently popular with
writers for children. This is a very fine
copy.

701 YOUTH'S INSTRUCTIVE AND ENTERTAINING
STORY-TELLER ; BEING A CHOICE COLLECTION
OF MORAL TALES ... Second edition, 12mo.
Newcastle upon Tyne, T. Saint, 1779. Hugo
15. First published 1774.

702 MORAL LECTURES, ON THE FOLLOWING SUB-
JECTS. PRIDE, ENVY [AND 26 OTHERS] ...
BY SOLOMON WINLOVE, ESQ. First edition,
16mo. *E. Newbery,* 1781. Extremely rare.
Welsh, pp. 331-2, quotes it only from

F. Newbery's list and as published without date. The 28 headpieces are by Bewick, but the earliest edition in Hugo is York 1803 (No. 190). A fine copy.

703 THE LIFE AND ADVENTURES OF A FLY. SUP-POSED TO HAVE BEEN WRITTEN BY HIMSELF. First edition, 12mo. *E. Newbery*, [1789]. Welsh p. 255 (quoted only from Newbery's list). Hugo, 4109. The frontispiece is signed by Bewick and some of the ten woodcuts are also by him.

704 REV. DR. TRUSLER. THE PROGRESS OF MAN AND SOCIETY ... First edition, sm. 8vo. *Printed for the Author*, 1791. Hugo (59). " With marvellously clever cuts by John Bewick."

705 THE ORACLES : CONTAINING SOME PARTICU-LARS OF THE HISTORY OF BILLY AND KITTY WILSON ... *Harris*, [*ca.* 1795]. Hugo (5391) lists what is presumably the first edition, published by Newbery without date. Welsh, p. 280, merely lists the title and says two of the cuts are by Bewick.

706 THE PICTURE ROOM ; CONTAINING THE ORIGINAL DRAWINGS OF EIGHTEEN LITTLE MASTERS AND MISSES ... *York : Wilson and Spence*, 1804. First edition, sq. 12mo. Hugo (194). With frontispiece and eighteen cuts by Bewick.

707 DIVINE SONGS, ATTEMPTED IN EASY LANGUAGE FOR THE USE OF CHILDREN. BY I. WATTS, D.D. *York : Wilson & Spence*, 1804. With 38 cuts by Bewick. The earliest edition

listed by Hugo with this title is his (5416);
but ours is doubtless a reprint of an edition
of 1804, with a slightly different title—
Hugo (4112).

708 CHARMS FOR CHILDREN ... First edition,
16mo. *York : Wilson and Spence*, 1806. Hugo
(4178). With a woodcut by Bewick to each
of the seven stories and J. Cresswell's Bewick
bookplate.

709 A SELECTION OF STORIES ; CONTAINING THE
HISTORY OF TWO SISTERS, THE FISHERMAN.
THE KING AND THE FAIRY RING, AND HONESTY
REWARDED. First edition, 24mo. *Glasgow :
Lumsden, ca.* 1814. Hugo (4266). With
J. Cresswell's Bewick bookplate. The legend
on the title-page " Embellished with Copper-
plates " is palpably false.

710 THE TRIUMPH OF GOOD NATURE, EXHIBITED IN
THE HISTORY OF MASTER HARRY FAIRBORN,
AND MASTER TRUEWORTH. First edition,
24mo. *Glasgow : Lumsden, ca.* 1814. Hugo
(314). Fourteen cuts by John Bewick.

711 THE PICTURE GALLERY. *Derby : Thomas
Richardson, ca.* 1820. This charming booklet
is not listed by Hugo. It was doubtless
hashed up by the publisher from a collection
of small blocks in his stock. Many of the
cuts are probably by other hands than
Bewick's.

712 TOM THUMB'S PLAY-BOOK, TO TEACH CHILDREN
THEIR LETTERS AS SOON AS THEY CAN SPEAK
... First edition, sq. 16mo. *Newcastle :
Bell*, 1874. An interesting example of the
way in which publishers made free with
Bewick's popularity. The covers of this

booklet consist of four cuts originally made
by Bewick for the *Select Fables* of 1784.   The
book includes two fables—" The Crow and
the Pitcher," and " The Two Frogs "—each
of which has a headpiece taken from Hastie's
" Reading Easy." The alphabet is illustrated from an old series of cuts not by
Bewick.

R. CALDECOTT

712a ORIGINAL DRAWINGS AND HAND-COLOURED
PROOFS FOR *The Farmer's Boy*. This collection consists of the original drawings for the
plates of horses, sheep, hens, and dogs, and
of proofs printed in outline of the other five
plates for the book, including the cover, in
each of which the artist has washed in the
colour as an indication to the printer of the
final appearance of the picture. The marginal comments in pencil shew the extreme
care with which Caldecott supervised the
production of his drawings.

712b ORIGINAL DRAWINGS AND HANDCOLOURED
PROOFS FOR *The Queen of Hearts*. This
collection consists of the original drawings
for the cover and the three heralds, and of
proofs printed in outline of the other seven
coloured plates for the book in each of which
the artist has washed in the colour as an
indication to the printer of the blocks
required to ·complete the final impression.
The marginal pencil marks are by Caldecott,
being directions to the blockmaker for the
blocks required to produce the finished
picture.

713 THE MILKMAID. AN OLD SONG... First
edition, oblong 8vo. *Routledge, ca.* 1880.

714 THE GREAT PANJANDRUM HIMSELF. First edition, oblong 8vo. *Routledge*, [1879].

715 THE THREE JOVIAL HUNTSMEN. First edition, sq. 8vo. *Routledge, ca.* 1880.

716 R. CALDECOTT'S PICTURE BOOK ... First miniature edition. *Routledge, ca.* 1890. After their separate issue at one shilling each, these immensely popular and successful books were gathered first into two volumes at five shillings each (*cf.* No. 717), then into a single volume costing half-a-guinea, and finally into two miniature volumes like this one, also at five shillings.

717 R. CALDECOTT'S PICTURE BOOK NO. 2. Second Collected edition. *Warne, ca.* 1900. Towards the end of the 19th century the association of the firm of Routledge with the long succession of children's books illustrated by Caldecott, Kate Greenaway, and others, came to an end. The Caldecott ' and Greenaway books were taken over by the firm of Warne, who re-issued them in the original form, engraved and printed by Edward Evans, whose perception and craftsmanship had first introduced Kate Greenaway to a wide public.

But there was a new star on the horizon and, by 1901, the names of Greenaway and Caldecott disappear from Warne's advertisements to be replaced by Beatrix Potter. (See Nos. 727-728f).

Exhibited with this is a proof of the cover design. This is pulled on a waste sheet on the back of which are two designs from *The Queen of Hearts*.

WALTER CRANE

718 THE OLD COURTIER. First edition, 8vo.
Routledge, ca. 1878. Crane's early form of
signature—a rebus of a crane—may be seen
in the lower right-hand corner of the cover
design. He collaborated with Kate
Greenaway in *The Quiver of Love* [1876],
and was almost as popular with children.

719 SLATEANDPENCILVANIA. First editiou, oblong
8vo. *Ward,* 1885.

719a STEPS TO READING. *Dent, ca.* 1895.

KATE GREENAWAY

719b, c & d. UNDER THE WINDOW. First edition,
8vo. *Routledge,* [1878]. This may reasonably
be regarded as Miss Greenaway's key book,
for it was the first to be produced by Edmund
Evans, and there is a good case to be made
for regarding the association with this great
engraver and printer as the real foundation
of all the artist's later successes. Previous
to the production of this work her illustrations were a secondary feature of the few
books in which they appeared : henceforth
the public came to look above all for her
name on a book. Evans took the greatest pains
with the production and with its background,
shewed the drawings and verse before publication to all and sundry—George Eliot and
Frederick Locker among others—and, defying
the pessimism of the publisher, insisted on
printing 20,000 copies of the first edition.
The French and German editions, which are
also shewn, were highly successful abroad.

720 MOTHER GOOSE OR THE OLD NURSERY RHYMES.
First edition, sm. 8vo. *Routledge,* [1881].
The description " first edition " as applied

to the books of Kate Greenaway should be regarded with the greatest caution. The variants have never been treated bibliographically, which is a great stumbling block to her many collectors. The present book, for example, exists with two entirely different covers and with no evidence of priority between them.

721 LITTLE ANN . . . First edition, 8vo. *Routledge*, [1882-3].

722 LANGUAGE OF FLOWERS. First edition, sm. sq. 8vo. *Routledge*, [1894].

722a, b and c. MARIGOLD GARDEN. First edition, 4to. *Routledge*, [1885]. This was only the second time that Miss Greenaway had ventured on authorship as well as illustration. It was successful : the first edition in England was 6,500, in the U.S.A. 7,500, and in France 3,500 copies—excellent figures for a book published at six shillings when children's books seldom exceeded half-a-crown in price. We include a proof copy before the text was added, a copy of the ordinary first edition and one of the first French edition.

723 THE ENGLISH SPELLING-BOOK . . . BY WILLIAM MAVOR. First edition, sm. 8vo. *Routledge*, 1885. This book had a curiously chequered career. In its original (present) form only 5,000 copies were sold. This, compared with over 70,000 of *Under the Window*, and 40,000 of her *Painting-Book*, spelt failure. The publishers re-issued the alphabet separately in a tiny 48mo volume and sold nearly 25,000 copies of it. Encouraged by this the illustrations for the *Almanack* of 1895 were taken entirely from the other drawings in " Mavor," but this was also a failure and was the last of the series and the last of Kate Greenaway's books to be issued by Routledge.

723a A PAINTING BOOK WITH OUTLINES FROM HER VARIOUS WORKS FOR GIRLS AND BOYS TO PAINT. First edition, 8vo. *Routledge*, [1885]. Although 40,000 copies were printed this is one of the hardest of the Greenaway books to find in pristine condition. The reason is obvious.

723b and c A—APPLE PIE. First edition, oblong 8vo. *Routledge*, [1886]. The · two copies shewn of this book illustrate the difficulty collectors have in identifying first editions of Miss Greenaway's works. There is not a pin to choose between them from a bibliographical point of view.

Ruskin disliked this version of an old favourite. He said the lettering was " billsticking of the vulgarest sort " and that, among the drawings, there was not one with " the least melodious charm." The feet were all " paddles or flappers."

723d THE QUEEN OF THE PIRATE ISLE. BY BRET HARTE. First edition, 8vo. *Chatto & Windus*, [1887]. This copy, being in the dustwrapper, shews just what a Greenaway book looked like when it was fresh from the publisher.

723e KATE GREENAWAY'S BOOK OF GAMES. First edition, 8vo. *Routledge*, [1889]. One of her happiest productions, because she was allowed to follow her own bent without consulting an author, the subject being one of her own choice and development. The first edition was of 10,000 copies.

723f GREENAWAY, CALDECOTT AND CRANE. ROUT-
LEDGE'S CHRISTMAS NUMBER. First edition,
8vo. [1881]. For the first and only time
the three famous illustrators appeared
together with one cover. All three plates
are shewn. Other illustrators included
Gustave Doré and Griset.

724 and 724a THE MAIDS OF LEE. THE MEN OF
WARE. WRITTEN BY F. E. WEATHERLY.
ILLUSTRATED BY W. J. HODGSON. *Published
by Hildesheimer and Faulkner*, [1883].
Between 1882 and 1889 Weatherley wrote
and Hildesheimer published thirty-three of
these derivations of Caldecott. In 1888
alone there were nine of them.

725 and 725a DREAMS, DANCES, AND DISAPPOINT-
MENTS. THE MAYPOLE. BY G. A. KONSTAM
AND E. AND N. CASTELLA. *De la Rue*, [1882].
Two typical endeavours to copy the
Greenaway manner.

726 THE DIVERTING HISTORY OF THREE BLIND
MICE. ILLUSTRATED BY E. CALDWELL. *Marcus
Ward*, [*ca.* 1890].

BEATRIX POTTER.

727 THE TALE OF PETER RABBIT.

(i) The privately printed edition, undated.
It is probable that this is a first finished copy
or final proof to show the general appearance
of the book. Bound in boards with a flat back.

(ii) The same but dated February, 1902, and
bound in stout boards with a rounded back.

(iii) The author's original manuscript of the
edition published by Warne later in 1902,
with proof pulls of the blocks, uncoloured,
pasted up as a dummy guide to the printer.

(iv) The author's original water-colour drawings of Warne's first edition. N.B.—The privately printed edition had only the frontispiece in colour. (See No. 728d).

This, the first of all the Beatrix Potter books, was begun in 1893, as one of a series of long illustrated letters written to some children who were friends of Miss Potter's. Other characters who later achieved fame were also mentioned in these letters, for example Mr. Jeremy Fisher. Canon Rawnsley and other friends urged her to try a publisher with a story based on these characters, and *Peter Rabbit* was the result. Warne and other publishers, to whom it was submitted, declined the book and the author had it printed at her own expense, drawing some of her savings from the Post Office to pay the bill. There were five hundred copies and she sold them to friends at one-and-twopence each, making, it is said, between £12 and £15 profit. If this is true the book cost only about £15 to produce, which is difficult to believe, even in 1902. The eventual result was of much greater importance, for Warne, having seen the book, decided to take the risk of a commercial edition and hundreds of thousands of children have blessed him for it.

728 THE TAILOR OF GLOUCESTER.

(i) The privately printed edition. *Christmas*, 1902.

(ii) The original manuscript of Warne's first edition, opened at page 7 to show an unused drawing.

Encouraged by the " success " of *Peter Rabbit* Miss Potter had already commissioned a similar printing of a second book, *The Tailor of Gloucester*. This time only four hundred copies were printed and we know that the cost was £40. Warne accepted this book also, but it was rewritten, shortened, and provided with new pictures for their edition. For this reason it was not published until after *Squirrel Nutkin*, which was thus the first book by Beatrix Potter actually commissioned by Warne. Both privately printed editions are now collector's treasures.

728a THE ROLY-POLY PUDDING. Publisher's dummy made up to show the author the layout of the text, so that she could plan the illustrations. The thumb-nail sketches shew her method of working. The book was originally published in approximately the same size as this dummy and with this title. When it assumed the familiar " dumpy " format its title was changed to *The Tale of Mr. Sammy Whiskers*.

728b THE TALE OF MR. BENJAMIN BUNNY. The first draft of the story written in " The Prince of Penny Exercise Books " with thumb-nail sketches suggesting the final drawings.

728c JOHNNY TOWN-MOUSE. Two original drawings for end-paper designs. One minor feature which shows the care and continued interest of the author in the production of her books is observable only in an extensive collection of them. The end-papers of her books are decorated with tiny pictures of Miss Potter's more popular characters. These were added to as the series grew and the two shewn were for a new volume. The bibliography of her books is complicated by the consequent variations in the end-paper.

728d CHRISTMAS CARD FOR INVALID CHILDREN'S AID ASSOCIATION. The original drawing and first and second proofs. Miss Potter took a keen interest in this Association and presented it with several designs for Christmas Cards, which were sold to raise funds. The present design is an adaptation of the original frontispiece to *Peter Rabbit*.

728e ANOTHER CHRISTMAS CARD FOR THE SAME FUND. The original drawing and the finished article.

728f BYAM SHAW. OLD KING COLE'S BOOK OF NURSERY RHYMES. 1901. A collection of 24 proof pulls of the woodblock illustrations for this book in each of which the artist has washed in the colours as a guide to the blockmakers in producing the finished pictures. The book was published by Macmillan, and the printing and blockmaking were the work of the firm of Edmund Evans and Son, printers of the work of Caldecott and Greenaway.

SECTION II : HIEROGLYPHIC BOOKS

729 SPECIMENS OF A SET OF HIEROGLYPHIC CARDS FOR CHILDREN. *Published by Wallis*, 1791.

730 THE ART OF MAKING MONEY PLENTY, IN EVERY MAN'S POCKET. BY DR. FRANKLIN. *Darton*, 1817. Engraved throughout, the story told in hieroglyphic form, with the correct reading at the foot of each page.

731 THE NEW AND INTERESTING GAME OF HIEROGLYPHICKS. *Gouyn*, 1826.

731a PETER THE PIEMAN. *Bellamy and Cooke*, ca. 1840.

732 FERONICA'S HIEROGLYPHICAL RIDDLES. *ca.* 1840. A guessing or interpreting game.

733 LETTERS BY CATHERINE SINCLAIR. *Edinburgh : James Wood, etc.,* 1863-1866. Six hieroglyphic letters in three parts. The first part was originally published in 1861. The indications of reprinting indicate their enormous success.

SECTION III : VARIOUS ILLUSTRATORS

734 YOUTH'S PASTIME. First edition, 16mo. *Sold in May's Buildings, Covent Garden, ca.* 1730. An extremely rare and hitherto apparently unrecorded work. The address is that of George Bickham, the famous eighteenth century engraver and calligrapher. This very crudely produced booklet can have added nothing to his reputation.

734a THE HISTORY AND DESCRIPTION OF THE FAMOUS CATHEDRAL OF ST. PAUL'S, LONDON. First edition, 2 vols., 32mo. *Printed for Tho. Boreman, Bookseller, near the two giants in Guildhall, London,* 1741. An extremely fine copy of this very rare miniature book. Illustrated with woodcuts. A list of juvenile subscribers in each volume. Note the queer imprint.

735 CHOICE EMBLEMS, NATURAL, HISTORICAL, FABULOUS, MORAL AND DIVINE, FOR THE IMPROVEMENT AND PASTIME OF YOUTH ... Sixth edition, fcap. 8vo. *E. Newbery,* 1788. This is the edition described by Welsh, p. 209. Engraved frontispiece and numerous cuts in the text.

736 THE WORLD TURNED UP-SIDE DOWN ; OR THE COMICAL METAMORPHOSES ... First edition, sq. 12mo. *Ryland,* [*ca.* 1790]. An extremely rare version, with engraved title and 31 (out of 32) full-page engravings.

737 THE WORLD TURNED UPSIDE-DOWN. First edition, sq. 12mo. *ca.* 1805. With 16 coloured plates with engraved verses below each.

738 THE WORLD TURNED UPSIDE DOWN ; OR, NO NEWS, AND STRANGE NEWS. *York : Kendrew,* [*ca.* 1820]. With numerous small woodcuts.

739 THE WORLD TURNED UPSIDE DOWN. FROM THE DESIGNS OF GIUSEPPI SALVIATI, ENGRAVED BY F. C. LEWIS. First edition, sq. 8vo. *Arch, etc.,* 1822. With 28 engravings and a verse to each.

740 A SET OF ALPHABETICAL CARDS EACH ILLUSTRATED WITH A WOODCUT IN THE BEWICK MANNER. [18*th century*].

741 HIEROGLYPHIC BIBLE (A CURIOUS) ; OR, SELECT PASSAGES IN THE OLD AND NEW TESTAMENTS, REPRESENTED WITH EMBLEMATICAL FIGURES, FOR THE AMUSEMENT OF YOUTH ... Ninth edition, sm. 8vo. *Hodgson,* 1791. The cuts have been attributed to Bewick and Hugo lists the above edition as his No. (61).

742 THE SLEEPING BEAUTY IN THE WOOD. *Plant, Sculpt.,* 1796.

743 THE CRIES OF LONDON ... *E. Newbery,* 1799.

744 EMBLEMS, FOR THE ENTERTAINMENT AND IMPROVEMENT OF YOUTH ; CONTAINING HIEROGLYPHICAL AND ENIGMATICAL DEVICES ... TOGETHER WITH EXPLANATIONS AND PROVERBS IN FRENCH, SPANISH, ITALIAN AND LATIN, ALLUDING TO THEM, AND TRANSLATED INTO ENGLISH : THE WHOLE CURIOUSLY ENGRAV'D ON 62 COPPER PLATES. First edition, sm. 8vo. *Sold by R. Ware at the Bible and Sun* ... [18*th century*].

744a PAINTING BOOKS FOR CHILDREN. Oblong
16mo. [*ca.* 1800]. Three very early painting books, with engravings in pairs, one
coloured, the other plain. Each in original
wrappers.

745 CHILDREN'S COPPER PLATE PICTURES. *Darton,
ca.* 1800-1825. A collection of 28 of these
sheets, each mounted on linen, as issued, sm.
folio. The early issues consist of one or two
large engraved scenes ; a set of four shipping
scenes ; another of four scenes on a farm, etc.
Nos. 29 and [30] are alphabets, one of flowers
and one of verses ; the remainder are small
engravings in " scrap " form, mostly 12 to a
sheet—topographical views, trades, birds,
games, etc.

746 MRS. LOVECHILD'S BOOK OF THREE HUNDRED
AND THIRTY-SIX CUTS FOR CHILDREN. *Darton,*
1801. Originally published in 1799.

747 DELIGHTFUL STORIES FOR GOOD CHILDREN :
CONSISTING OF THE MOUNTAIN LUTE, THE
LITTLE ISLANDERS, THE YOUNG ROBBER, THE
CONJURING BIRD, THE MILITARY ACADEMY,
THE TAME GOLDFINCH. First edition, 12mo.
Harris, 1804. Each story has a separate
title-page and is illustrated with 3 engravings,
which indicate that they may have been
issued separately.

748 THE ORIGINAL DRAWINGS FOR THE ILLUSTRA-
TIONS TO *Delightful Stories. Published by
Harris in* 1804 (No. 747).

748a SEVENTY-EIGHT QUIZZICAL CHARACTERS, FOR
THE AMUSEMENT OF CHILDREN. BY DAME
PASTIME. *B. Blake, ca.* 1805. Twelve full-
page coloured plates with engraved captions.
Blake's publications are rather rare.

749 " BURDEKIN SHEETS." A REMARKABLE COL-
LECTION OF 28 SHEETS OF WOODCUTS FOR
CHILDREN. *Published by R. Burdekin, High
Ousegate, York,* [*ca.* 1805]. This series of
sheets, each containing from 4 to 12 woodcuts, were one of the earliest forms of scraps
for children to cut out and stick in albums.
Many of the cuts are by Bewick. The series
is numbered from 5 to 32 inclusive.

750 THE TALKING BIRD : OR, DAME TRUDGE AND
HER PARROT. First edition, sq. 12mo.
Harris, 1806. With 16 full-page engravings.

751 THE ORIGINAL DRAWINGS FOR *The Talking
Bird. Published by J. Harris,* 1806. (No.
750).

752 THE MAGIC LANTERN ; OR, AMUSING AND
INSTRUCTIVE EXHIBITIONS FOR YOUNG PEOPLE
First edition, sm. 8vo. *Tabart,* [*ca.* 1806].
A very fine copy of a beautiful book, with
11 charming coloured engravings each illus-
trating one evening's entertainment.

752a PUG'S VISIT OR THE DISASTERS OF MR. PUNCH.
12mo. *Harris, April* 20*th,* 1806. With 16
full-page engravings.

752b SIX OF THE ORIGINAL WATER-COLOUR DRAW-
INGS FOR *Pug's Visit.* (No. 752a).

753 MEMOIRS OF THE LITTLE MAN AND THE LITTLE
MAID ... *Tabart,* 1808. With 12 pages of
engraved words and music, 12 hand-coloured
engravings and 2 pages list of Tabart's
publications.

754 MOUNSEER NONGTONGPAW : A NEW VERSION.
Proprietors of the Juvenile Library, 41, *Skinner
St.,* 1808. With 12 coloured engravings.

755 PETER PRIM'S PRIDE, OR PROVERBS THAT WILL SUIT THE YOUNG, OR THE OLD. First edition, sq. 12mo. *Harris*, 1810. Engraved throughout, with 15 charming coloured engravings.

756 HODGE, HIS WIFE, AND HIS TWO BOYS. A MORAL TALE. First edition, sq. 12mo. *Lee & Walker*, 1810. With 16 woodcuts.

756a THE HAPPY COURTSHIP, MERRY MARRIAGE, AND PIC-NIC DINNER, OF COCK ROBIN, AND JENNY WREN. TO WHICH IS ADDED, ALAS ! THE DOLEFUL DEATH OF THE BRIDEGROOM. *Harris*, 1814. For this edition Harris resurrected the plates of the 1806 edition (see Nos. 307 and 308), but they were by this time so badly worn that they reproduced not much more than the outlines. He therefore commissioned nine new drawings. (See No. 756b).

756b THE NINE ORIGINAL DRAWINGS FOR THE 1814 EDITION OF *Cock Robin*. (No. 756a).

757 THE SHEPHERD BOY. *W Cole*, [*ca.* 1815]. Engraved throughout, with title and 11 tiny plates with a verse to each.

758 THREE PICTURE BOOKS FOR CHILDREN ... FROM ENGRAVINGS ON COPPER. *Alnwick* : *W. Davison, ca.* 1815. These plates are not numbered consecutively : they were probably taken from a larger publication, or possibly issued as separate picture sheets.

759 VICISSITUDE : OR THE LIFE AND ADVENTURES OF NED FROLIC. AN ORIGINAL COMIC SONG, FOR THE ENTERTAINMENT OF ALL GOOD BOYS AND GIRLS IN THE BRITISH EMPIRE. First edition, 12mo. *Glasgow* : *Lumsden*, 1818. With frontispiece and 3 engravings containing 21 miniature illustrations, all coloured.

760 THE PICTURE SHOP FOR GOOD CHILDREN. First edition, oblong 12mo. *Darton*, [ca. 1820]. This consists entirely of 32 engravings, with alphabets at the beginning and end.

761 ELIZABETH ; OR, THE EXILES OF SIBERIA: TRANSLATED FROM THE FRENCH OF MADAME COTTIN. *Hodgson, ca.* 1820. A well-known "Gothic" romance.

762 TOMMY TRIP'S MUSEUM ; OR A PEEP AT THE QUADRUPED RACE. *Harris, ca.* 1820.

763 BELCH'S ENTERTAINING VIEWS. First edition, sm. 8vo. *Printed, Published and Sold by W. Belch, ca.* 1825. With 8 half-page coloured engravings.

764 CAUTIONARY STORIES, CONTAINING THE DAISY AND COWSLIP, ADAPTED TO THE IDEAS OF CHILDREN FROM FOUR TO EIGHT YEARS OLD. *Harris*, 1825. Written by Elizabeth Turner, originally published in 1807, and provided with new illustrations for this edition.

765 ORIGINAL DRAWINGS FOR HARRIS'S 1825 EDITION OF *The Daisy*, BY ELIZABETH TURNER (No. 764).

766 EARLY IMPRESSIONS ; OR MORAL AND IN-STRUCTIVE ENTERTAINMENT FOR CHILDREN IN PROSE AND VERSE. First edition, sm. 8vo. *Hatchard*, 1828. With 12 charming lithographs by Dighton. An early example of lithography.

767 SCENES IN BRIGHTON, HANDSOMELY COLOURED First edition, sm. 8vo. *Hodgson*, [ca. 1830]. With eight coloured views of Brighton, each with descriptive verse beneath.

768 DRUNKEN BARNABY AND SCOLDING MARGERY. *Dean and Munday*, [*ca.* 1825]. With seven coloured engravings by R. Stennett. A highly unsuitable book for children.

769 MARY ELLIOTT. EARLY SEEDS TO PRODUCE SPRING FLOWERS. *Darton, ca.* 1825.

770 ROSAMOND. DOLLY'S NEW PICTURE BOOK. TRANSLATED FROM THE GERMAN OF MADAME DE CHATELAINE. Oblong 32mo. *Stuttgart and London* : *Thienemann & Myers*, [*ca.* 1840]. With 16 charming full-page coloured illustrations by Rudolph Geissler, shewing incidents in a doll's life. The original was probably German.

771 NEW AND ORIGINAL POEMS, WITH NOTES, ON CREATION AND REDEMPTION, BY E. SHILLITO, ENTITLED THE FOOTSTEPS OF JESUS, COMPRISING THE HISTORY OF ADAM AND EVE . . . First edition, cr. 8vo. *Hull* : *Author*, [*ca.* 1840]. Chiefly interesting as a specimen of printing. Some leaves on coloured paper, some in gold and some in colour. Numerous cuts by Bewick. The verse is the work of a religious fanatic and the entire production is extremely odd.

772 A. DUMAS. THE HISTORY OF A NUTCRACKER. WITH 220 ILLUSTRATIONS BY BERTALL. PART I. First English edition, sm. 8vo. *Chapman and Hall*, 1847. Coloured lithograph frontispiece.

773 HARRY'S LADDER TO LEARNING. (1) HARRY'S HORNBOOK, (2) HARRY'S PICTURE BOOK, (3) HARRY'S NURSERY SONGS, (4) HARRY'S SIMPLE STORIES. First editions, 4 in 1 vol., sm. sq. 8vo. *Bogue*, 1849. With about 180 charming coloured illustrations.

774 AUNT MARY'S NEW YEAR'S GIFT. FOR LITTLE BOYS AND GIRLS WHO ARE LEARNING TO READ. *Darton, ca.* 1850. With chromolithograph title, four full-page coloured plates and numerous cuts in the text.

775 PICTURES OF TRAVEL AND ADVENTURE. *ca.* 1850. A series of 7 coloured lithographs opening in panorama form.

776 GEORGE CRUIKSHANK'S FAIRY LIBRARY. HOP-O'-MY-THUMB AND THE SEVEN-LEAGUE BOOTS ... First edition, sm. 4to. *Bogue,* [1853].

777 THREE LITTLE KITTENS. BY COMUS ... 4to. *Nelson,* 1859.

778 LITTLE STORIES FOR LITTLE READERS. (2) THE CHEERFUL COMPANION, AN EASY STORY BOOK FOR YOUNG CHILDREN. Two in 1 vol., cr. 8vo. *Darton, ca.* 1860. Both illustrated in oil by G. C. Leighton, a Baxter licensee.

779 FAVOURITE SONGS FOR CHILDREN, FROM DR. WATTS. *Webb, Millington,* [*ca.* 1865].

780 E. V. B[OYLE]. CHILD'S PLAY. First edition, sq. 8vo. *Sampson Low,* 1865. Numerous full-page coloured plates.

781 WARNE'S PICTURE PUZZLE TOY BOOK ... *Warne, ca.* 1865. The pictures are partly printed in colours, but with spaces left in white. The missing portions were found on a sheet in a pocket at the front of the book, to be cut out and pasted on by the children.

782 D. W. THOMPSON. FUN AND EARNEST; OR, RHYMES WITH REASON. First edition, cr. 8vo. *Griffith and Farran,* 1865. Coloured illustrations by C. H. Bennett.

783 C. H. ROSS. MERRY CONCEITS AND WHIMSICAL RHYMES. First edition, cr. 8vo. *Routledge,* 1866. Coloured plates by the author.

784 BRITISH SOLDIERS. *Routledge, ca.* 1865.

784 A DISSERTATION UPON ROAST PIG BY CHARLES LAMB. WITH ILLUSTRATIONS BY C. O. MURRAY. *Sampson, Low, ca.* 1880.

785 MARCUS WARD'S JAPANESE PICTURE STORIES. ABOU-HASSAN . . . *Ward, ca.* 1880.

SECTION IV : **MOVEABLE BOOKS**

Ingenuity of invention in the entertainment of children has seldom been more indulged than in the books shewn in this small section. Anyone who has tried to repair or to imitate one of the Meggendorfer series (Nos. 808 to 810) must marvel no less at the complicated nature of its " works " than at the possibility of producing them by hand at a price commensurate with the children's market. Sweated labour is the solution of that, of course.

If the sophisticated modern, on examining No. 809, in which the " works " are exposed to view, is tempted to observe that the resulting movement is as a mole-hill to a mountain, he should reflect that the cheap clockwork toys of their own youth hardly pre-date the twentieth century. Mechanical toys certainly existed before that date, but they were very expensive. At the Great Exhibition of 1851, for example, a clockwork stage-carriage cost £2 8s. 0d., at least three times as much translated into our currency. As against this dressed dolls were offered at eightpence a dozen and undressed composition. dolls at only *two-pence-halfpenny a dozen* !

The attraction for children of any toy that can be made to move is not new but it was not until about 1840 that anything sufficiently compact to be issued within covers was devised. (See Nos. 798 to 815). Prior to this date ingenuity was confined to the charming series of cut-out figures issued by S. and J. Fuller (Nos. 786 to 794) which were enormously successful for at least twenty years. They were soon copied in France and Germany : some of the English stories were translated for the purpose. This series is clearly the forerunner of the doll-dressing cards which still entertain modern children.

786 THE HISTORY AND ADVENTURES OF LITTLE HENRY ... *S. & J. Fuller*, 1810. In the early nineteenth century there were more shops catering exclusively for children than there are now, and S. and J. Fuller's Temple of Fancy in Rathbone Place was not the least important or enterprising. This series of books with coloured cut-out figures and interchangeable heads originated with them.

786a THE HISTORY OF LITTLE HENRY ... 1830. This shows the continued interest in this series twenty years after its inception. A catalogue at the end of the book lists most of the series and also advertises the panoramas and peep-shows in which Fuller's also specialized.

787 ELLEN, OR THE NAUGHTY GIRL RECLAIMED ... *S. and J. Fuller*, 1811. Note the various hats on some of the figures.

788 HISTORY OF LITTLE FANNY ... *S. and J. Fuller*, 1811

789 PHOEBE, THE COTTAGE MAID ... *S. and J. Fuller*, 1811. It is perhaps significant of the sophistication of the small patrons of the Temple of Fancy that, despite the greater elaboration of the cut-outs, this book seems to have been a comparative failure. This may be deduced from its much greater rarity and from the fact that it does not seem to have been reprinted. Its sequel, *Hubert, the Cottage Boy*, I have never seen. It also was a failure.

790 FRANK FEIGNWELL'S ATTEMPTS TO AMUSE HIS FRIENDS ON TWELFTH NIGHT. *S. and J. Fuller*, 1811.

791 YOUNG ALBERT, THE ROSCIUS ... *S. and J. Fuller*, 1811. This is an aftermath of the meteoric career of William Betty (Beatty ?), the young Roscius, who, at the age of thirteen, starred at Covent Garden and Drury Lane Theatres. The takings at Drury Lane averaged over £600 a night for twenty-eight nights in his first season, and Pitt adjourned the House of Commons in order that members might attend his performance of Hamlet. Betty died in 1874 aged eighty-two, having retired from the stage fifty years before.

792 CINDERELLA ; OR THE LITTLE GLASS SLIPPER ... *S. and J. Fuller*, 1814. One of the last, most elaborate and most charming of this series.

793 LE JEU DES FABLES, OU FABLES DE LAFON- TAINE MISES EN ACTION, AVEC FIGURES COLORIÉES ET DÉCOUPÉES, DESSINÉES ET GRAVÉES PAR LAMBERT ÂINÉ. *A Paris, chez L'Auteur ... ca.* 1815. Figures from the envelope are inserted in the appropriate slits in the background in accordance with the plans at the end of the book. Thirty-five figures are provided to illustrate fifteen fables.

794 FABLES IN ACTION, BY MEANS OF SMALL MOVEABLE PICTURES AND DISSECTED AND COLOURED FIGURES . . . *Ackermann*, 1819. An English adaptation of No. 793. The pocket for the figures, the background, and the key are here ingeniously combined.

795 THE TOILET. Third edition, sq. 12mo. *Author, etc.*, 1823. With engraved frontispiece and 9 coloured engravings with moveable flaps, shewing articles from a lady's dressing table. When lifted a moral motto is disclosed : thus, " Best white paint " proves to be " Innocence." First published in 1821.

796 TOILET. *Rock Brothers & Payne, ca.* 1845. With coloured title and nine coloured plates, with moveable flaps. A new version of No. 795.

797 [STACEY GRIMALDI]. A SUIT OF ARMOUR FOR YOUTH. First edition, sm. 8vo. *Published by the Proprietor*, 1824. With engraved frontispiece and a series of 11 engravings of pieces of armour as moveable flaps, with other moral engravings beneath, thus, beneath " A Noble Helmet " is a scene depicting " Wisdom," etc.

798 THE VOYAGES AND ADVENTURES OF ROBINSON CRUSOE. [? *Dean, ca.* 1840]. On each page is an illustration similar to the one shewn which is erected by pulling a ribbon attached to the book.

799 CENDRILLON OU LA PETITE PANTOUFLE DE VERRE. *Paris*: *Magnin, ca.* 1840.

800 LAMPART'S ZWEITES LEBENDIGES BILDERBUCH MIT BEWEGLICHEN FIGUREN ZUR BELUSTIGUNG FÜR KINDER. *Augsburg*: *Lampart, ca.* 1840.

801 DEAN'S NEW BOOK OF DISSOLVING VIEWS. *Dean, ca.* 1850. By pulling the tab below each picture " dissolves " into another. The exhibit shews " Earth " on the right and " Air " (the second picture of this pair) on the left.

802 A VISIT TO THE EXHIBITION IN EIGHT CHANGEABLE PICTURES. SHOWING ITS BEAUTIFUL OBJECTS OF ART, AND HOW THEY WERE MADE. *Dean*, [1862]. Each page represents a stall at the Exhibition and the pulling of the tab discloses the workshops in which the exhibits were made.

803 THE HISTORY OF HOW NED NIMBLE BUILT HIS COTTAGE. *Dean, ca.* 1865.

804 THE FARMER AND HIS FAMILY. *Dean, ca.* 1865.

805 MOVEABLE SHADOWS. BY W. NEWMAN (OF " PUNCH "). *Dean, ca.* 1870. By pulling the tab each figure discloses a disrespectful form of its shadow.

806 PUSS IN BOOTS. *Dean, ca.* 1870. One of a series of five books in which a small change is made in the illustrations when each of the flaps is turned. These were the " Pantomime Toy Books."

807 DADDY'S GONE A-HUNTING. A TALE BY AUNT FANNY. *Dean, ca.* 1870. One of a series similar to the foregoing, called the " Changing Panoramic Toy Books."

808 ZUM ZEITVERTREIB FÜR BRAVE KNABEN & MÄDCHEN. EIN ZIEHBILDERBUCH VON LOTHAR MEGGENDORFER. *München : Braun und Schneider, ca.* 1880. This and the two following books are examples of the famous " Meggendorfers." This ingenious designer, by an extremely complicated arrangement of strips of thin cardboard joined to each other and to the operating tab (see No. 809), succeeded in producing an elaboration of movement in his pictures which has never been surpassed and is probably unequalled in its kind.

809 NAH UND FERN. EIN TIERBILDERBUCH ZUM ZIEHEN VON L. MEGGENDORFER. *München : Braun und Schneider, ca.* 1880. In this example the back of one of the pictures is exposed, shewing the complexity of the " mechanism."

810 SCENES IN THE LIFE OF A MASHER. A MOVE-ABLE TOYBOOK BY LOTHAR MEGGENDORFER. *H. Grevel & Co., ca.* 1885. Most of the series were issued in English as well as in German ; they were, however, produced in Germany under the supervision of their designer.

811 PASTIME PICTURES. *Nister, ca.* 1890. This and the following four books were published in London by a branch of the Munich firm of Nister. The extreme ingenuity of many of the devices used was matched by their careful study of the English market. Thus, the present book has verses by Clifton Bingham and the subjects include the Crystal Palace, the Zoo, etc. The method is similar to that used in Dean's Dissolving Views. (No. 801).

812 THE MAGIC TOY BOOK. *Nister, ca.* 1895.
By holding each picture to a strong light the
scene on the reverse shows through creating
a change of incident.

813 IN WONDER LAND. A BOOK OF REVOLVING
PICTURES. *Nister, ca.* 1900. By revolving
the silk tab the picture disappears and an
entirely different one replaces it.

814 MAGIC MOMENTS. VERSES BY CLIFTON
BINGHAM. PEN AND INK ILLUSTRATIONS BY
FLORENCE HARDY. *Nister, ca.* 1900. Similar
in action to No. 813.

815 RAILWAY PICTURES. A PANORAMA BOOK FOR
CHILDREN. VERSES BY SHEILA BRAINE.
Nister, ca. 1900.

SECTION V :

HARLEQUINADES or "TURN-UPS."

Robert Sayer appears to have been the first
to publish this curious form of picture book.
There is reason to presume their comparative
lack of success. He published fifteen of them,
of which we are able to include eleven. All of
these are listed in Laurie and Whittle's catalogue
of 1795 at prices reduced from sixpence plain or
one shilling coloured, to four shillings and eight
shillings a dozen respectively. It is perhaps
significant that this offer is in wholesale form
only.

Furthermore, the success of a new idea in
juvenile literature was the signal for piracy,
copying and adaptations of all kinds by other

booksellers ; this was singularly little in evidence in harlequinades. The common name for them, according to the Laurie and Whittle catalogue, was " Turn Ups."

816 THE FAIRY KING. *ca.* 1750 (?). The lower flap of the first picture is missing ; it probably included an imprint and date. The date given here is taken from Sotheby's catalogue.

817 [THE KING AND THE CLOWN]. *Sayer*, 1767. Robert Sayer took over the old-established business of the Overtons. Philip Overton's shop in Fleet Street is mentioned in Gay's " Trivia." He was, in turn, taken over by Laurie & Whittle. The title of the Harlequinade is taken from the catalogue of their publications issued in 1795 by this firm. The legend " Book 2 " in the lower left-hand corner of the first page does not denote that this is a sequel, but that it is second in Sayer's series of Harlequinades.

818 and 818a HARLEQUIN'S INVASION. A NEW PANTOMIME ... *Sayer*, 1770. The possession of a duplicate of this book permits the showing of the centre pages both closed and open. No. 4 of Sayer's series.

819 JOBSON AND NELL OR, THE WIVES METAMORPHOS'D. *Sayer*, 1770. No. 5 of Sayer's series.

820 QUEEN MAB OR THE TRICKS OF HARLEQUIN ... *Sayer*, 1771. No. 6 of Sayer's series.

820a and 820b MOTHER SHIPTON OR HARLEQUIN IN DESPAIR. PARTS I AND II. *Sayer*, 1771. Nos 7 and 9 of Sayer's series.

821 and 821a THE ELOPEMENT: A NEW HARLE-
QUIN ENTERTAINMENT ... *Sayer*, 1771. No.
8 of Sayer's series, published between the two
parts of Mother Shipton. Here again we are
able to show the flaps open and closed.

822 DR. LAST OR THE DEVIL UPON TWO STICKS.
Sayer, 1771. No. 11 in Sayer's series.

823 THE COMICAL TRICKS OF JACK THE PIPER ...
H. Roberts and L. Tomlinson, 1772. Highly
unsuitable for children; each incident is
concerned with the frailty of friars.

824 HARLEQUIN CHEROKEE OR THE INDIAN CHIEFS
IN LONDON. *Sayer*, 1772. No. 12 in Sayer's
series.

825 HARLEQUIN SKELETON. *Sayer*, 1772. No.
13 in Sayer's series.

826 THE CHIMNEY SWEEPER, A SIMILE. *Sayer*,
1772. No. 15 in Sayer's series.

827 THE PENMAN'S DIVERSION. 1776. An extremely curious home-made example. (*Cf.*
Nos. 833 and 834).

828 FALSHOOD OF EXTERNAL APPEARANCES. *ca.*
1775.

829 A NEW HARLEQUIN. THE OSTRICH EGG. *Laurie
& Whittle*, 1798.

830 HARLEQUIN'S HABEAS, AS PERFORMED AT THE
THEATRE ROYAL, COVENT GARDEN. *T. Hughes*,
1803. The first, and so far as we are aware,
the only example of a grandiloquent scheme
of Hughes's, agencies for which were taken by
Harris, Champante & Whitrow and others.
The series was called " The Juvenile Theatre,"
and was to consist of " Dramatic Delinea-
tions ... of all the most Favourite Spectacles,

Pantomimes, Ballets," etc., at the principal theatres ; possibly an abortive forerunner of the juvenile drama.

831 TWO SETS OF DRAWINGS FOR AN UNPUBLISHED (?) HARLEQUINADE. The paper is watermarked 1804.

832 EXILE, AS PERFORMED AT THE ROYAL THEATRES. *Tabart*, 1809.

833 METAMORPHOSIS ; OR, A TRANSFORMATION OF PICTURES ... *New York : Samuel Wood*, 1816. We can show no printed English harlequinade on these lines ; but it is very striking that two MS. specimens (Nos. 827 and 834) follow an exactly similar theme. In Laurie & Whittle's catalogue of 1795, however, there is one called *Adam and Eve*, which was probably of this kind.

834 AN ORIGINAL MANUSCRIPT HARLEQUINADE on the same theme as Nos. 827 and 833. The paper is watermarked 1830.

SECTION VI : RAG BOOKS

835 UNCLE BUNCLE'S GOOD LITTLE BOY. *Dean and Munday*, *ca.* 1830. An early and rather crude attempt at preparing indestructible books. The ordinary printed sheet is pasted to a piece of book cloth.

836 BOWDEN'S INDESTRUCTIBLE BATTLEDORE. *Gainsborough : J. W. Bowden, ca.* 1845. The make-up of this battledore is as follows : the cover sheet is printed on paper, the interior on linen ; between these are a sheet of paper and a sheet of thin card.

837 THE HISTORY OF THE HOUSE THAT JACK BUILT. *Griffith & Farran, ca.* 1850. Printed in colours on paper which is mounted on linen. Frontispiece and 14 illustrations in colour.

838 THE OLD WOMAN AND HER PIG. *Griffith & Farran, ca.* 1850. Similar technique to No. 837.

839 and 839a THE STORY OF DAME FORTUNE'S MAGIC WHEEL. THE STORY OF THE INDIANS AND THE BOX OF BEADS. *Wheeler,* 1852. Two of a series of four, printed on linen without reinforcement.

840 BERTIE'S TREASURY WITH MORE THAN ONE HUNDRED PICTURES. *Bogue,* [1853]. A very fine specimen of an early indestructible book, the text and pictures actually printed on linen of better and stronger quality than Nos. 839 and 839a.

841 THE A B C BOOK. WITH 8 PICTURES. *Ward & Lock, ca.* 1853. The earliest example we can shew of printing in colours on linen.

842 THE CHILD'S EASY LESSON BOOK. *Dean,* [1857].

43 THE CHILD'S OWN ALPHABET. WITH 24 PICTURES. *Low,* [*ca.* 1860].

844 LITTLE DOG BOB AND HIS FRIENDS. *Darton, ca.* 1865. A return to an earlier technique— text and pictures printed on paper and mounted on coarse linen.

PART V

Binding Styles

This small section covers very briefly and inadequately the changes in binding styles over the period from Newbery's earliest beginnings to the end of the nineteenth century. It is not uninteresting to compare this part of the exhibition with Part IV, which covers the evolution of illustration over the same period.

845 J. NEWBERY. 1762.

846 NEWBERY AND CARNON. 1768.

847 F. NEWBERY. 1777.

848 R. BASSAM. *ca.* 1780.

849 ANONYMOUS. *ca.* 1790.

850 MARSHALL. *ca.* 1785.

851 COLLINS OF SALISBURY. 1790.

852 ANONYMOUS. *ca.* 1790.

853 LUCKMAN AND SUFFIELD OF COVENTRY.

854 HOLLIS. *ca.* 1800.

855 A MODERN " RECONSTRUCTION."

856 CALF IN ABOUT 1772.

857 SHEEPSKIN. 1777.

858 RUSSIA. 1792.

859 MOROCCO, ABOUT 1830.

860 A SCHOOL PRIZE BINDING OF 1653.

861 OSBORNE & GRIFFIN. *ca.* 1785.

862 WATTS & BRIDGEWATER. *ca.* 1790.

863 DARTON. 1811.

864 and 864a AN INTERESTING EXAMPLE OF "SECONDARY" BINDING. The original is of 1818, with a picture of Harris's shop on the cover. 864a has the same sheets, still dated 1818, but the binding is of the late 1830's.

865 HOULSTON OF WELLINGTON ABOUT 1820. A typical chap-book cover.

866 DEAN & MUNDAY. *ca.* 1830.

867 TILT. 1838.

868 TAYLOR OF BRIGHTON. 1839.

869 WRIGHT. 1848.

870 R.T.S. *ca.* 1850.

871 DEAN. *ca.* 1855.

872 DEAN. *ca.* 1865.

873 DARTON. *ca.* 1865.

874 ROUTLEDGE. [1881].

875 TUCK. *ca.* 1890.

PART VI

Periodicals

Sporadic attemps were made in the eighteenth century to issue periodicals for children. Two of these and an offshoot of a third are shewn here, but it is extremely doubtful whether either of the first two items (Nos. 876 and 877) was actually issued in periodical form. Marshall's *Children's Magazine* (No. 878), however, was certainly a regular monthly publication during its short lifetime, and he also issued *The Juvenile Magazine*, which comprised twelve monthly parts.

It is worth noting that eighteenth century part issues were rather more successful than periodicals. Berquin's *L'Ami des Enfants* (No. 454) ran for more than two years in monthly parts, but this was rather more akin to the nineteenth century part-issues of novels by Dickens, Thackeray and others than to a magazine as we understand it.

One of the earliest of consistently successful magazines for children was *Little Folks* (No. 882).

876 LILLIPUTIAN POETRY : CONTAINING ALL THE MORAL AND ENTERTAINING POEMS PUBLISHED IN THE LILLIPUTIAN MAGAZINE . . . BY CHRISTOPHER CRAMBO, ESQ. : POET LAUREATE TO THE KING OF LILLIPUT . . . First edition, 12mo. *Tringham, etc.*, [*ca.* 1760].
This publication appears to have no connection with Newbery's *Lilliputian Magazine* (see No. 877).

877 THE LILLIPUTIAN MAGAZINE : OR, THE YOUNG GENTLEMAN'S GOLDEN LIBRARY. BEING AN ATTEMPT TO MEND THE WORLD . . . *Carnan*, 1783. The original issue of this book was advertised for publication in monthly numbers in 1751, but no set nor any single example of such publication is extant.

878 THE CHILDREN'S MAGAZINE ; OR MONTHLY REPOSITORY OF INSTRUCTION AND DELIGHT. NOS. 1 to 6, the separate parts bound with a general engraved title, 12mo. *Marshall, Jan. to June*, 1799. One of the earliest attempts at a periodical for children. Each part included an engraved plate and a map on " Patent Coloured Paper."

879 THE PICTURE MAGAZINE, OR MONTHLY EXHIBITION FOR YOUNG PEOPLE. VOL. III. First edition, sq. 12mo. *Marshall*, 1800-01. With 44 full-page coloured engravings.

880 FISHER'S JUVENILE SCRAP-BOOK. [EDITED] BY BERNARD BARTON. *Fisher*, 1836. An annual miscellany of verse and prose in the style of the " Keepsake " series, which was continued until 1850. This copy bears a presentation inscription in verse from the editor.

881 FISHER'S JUVENILE SCRAP-BOOK. [EDITED] BY AGNES STRICKLAND AND BERNARD BARTON. *Fisher*, 1838. The third annual volume. In this example all the plates are coloured.

882 LITTLE FOLKS : A MAGAZINE FOR THE YOUNG. *Cassell*, [1870]. The first volume of a famous magazine for children.

PART VII

American Juveniles

883 THE HISTORY OF MASTER JACKEY AND MISS HARRIOT : TOGETHER WITH A FEW MAXIMS FOR THE IMPROVEMENT OF THE MIND. DEDICATED TO GOOD CHILDREN OF THE UNITED STATES OF AMERICA. *Boston : Printed and Sold by Samuel Hall, No. 53, Cornhill,* 1791. Illustrated with numerous small woodcuts. An extremely fine copy and extremely rare. Not in Rosenbach, who records only three books published by Hall.

884 FAMILIAR DIALOGUES FOR THE INSTRUCTION AND AMUSEMENT OF CHILDREN OF FOUR AND FIVE YEARS OLD. *Boston [Mass.] : Hall & Hiller,* 1804. Extremely rare. Not in Rosenbach.

885 THE AMERICAN TOILET. Second edition, sq. 12mo. *New York : Imbert's Lithographic Office,* [*ca.* 1825]. A fine copy, with 20 lithographic illustrations, each of an article from a lady's dressing-table, with a moveable flap which, when raised, discloses a pious or moral message ; thus a glass bowl headed "A Wash to Smooth Wrinkles," shows, when its cover is lifted " Contentment " ; " Best White Paint " is " Innocence " ; and so on. An exact copy of No. 795.

886 BUNYAN'S PILGRIM'S PROGRESS, FROM THIS WORLD TO THAT WHICH IS TO COME, EXHIBITED IN A METAMORPHOSIS ... *Designed and Published by J. W. Barber, Hartford,* 1821.

886a ———— ANOTHER EDITION, CALLED " THE FOURTH." *New Haven, Ct.* : *G. Barber,* 1840. The later edition has a new set of cuts : both editions are on the harlequinade system.

887 THE ADVENTURES OF GENERAL BEAUREGARD AND HIS CHARGER. IN FOUR PARTS ILLUS-TRATED. *Phila* : *Samuel C. Upham,* [1861]. A modern photographic facsimile from the original in the Emmet Collection.

PART VIII

A Short History of a Famous Publisher

This is an all too inadequate attempt to illustrate the publishing history of the most famous of all publishers for children. The name of John Newbery is immortalized in the memory of everyone who studies the evolution of juvenile literature. No attempt is made here to enlarge on his importance, nor to suggest even the barest details of his history. The frequent appearance of his imprint throughout this catalogue is evidence of his high standing. The imprints shewn here give some notion of the apostolic succession of the later years of the firm.

888 J. NEWBERY. [1751].

889 F. NEWBERY. 1775.

890 E. NEWBERY. [1787].

891 E. NEWBERY. 1788.

892 E. NEWBERY. 1789.

893 E. NEWBERY. 1794.

894 J. HARRIS. 1808.

895 J. HARRIS. [1816].

896 J. HARRIS. [1817].

897 J. HARRIS. [1821].

898 J. HARRIS & SON. 1823.

899 J. HARRIS & SON. 1824.

900 J. HARRIS. 1825.

901 J. HARRIS. [1827].

902 J. HARRIS. 1834.

903 GRANT & GRIFFITH. *ca.* 1835.

904 GRIFFITH, FARRAN, OKEDEN & WELSH. [1883].

PART IX

Children's Games

SECTION I: OUTDOOR GAMES

905 JACQUES STELLA. LES JEUX ET PLAISIRS DE L'ENFANCE. First edition, oblong 4to. *Paris, aux Galleries du Louvre chez la ditte Stella,* 1657. 51 engraved plates, including title, of children at play, with verses to each.

906 THE ADVENTURES OF A WHIPPING-TOP. ILLUSTRATED WITH STORIES OF MANY BAD BOYS, WHO THEMSELVES DESERVE WHIPPING, AND OF SOME GOOD BOYS, WHO DESERVE PLUM PUDDING. First edition, 16mo. *Marshall,* ca. 1780. Frontispiece and 21 woodcuts.

907 RATIONAL SPORTS. IN DIALOGUES PASSING AMONG THE CHILDREN OF A FAMILY ... First edition, sm. 8vo. *Marshall,* ca. 1783.

908 THE BOOK OF GAMES; OR A HISTORY OF THE JUVENILE SPORTS, PRACTISED AT THE KINGSTON ACADEMY. First edition, 12mo. *Tabart,* 1805. With 24 hand-coloured engravings of boys, games, the frontispiece being Cricket.

909 RURAL SPORTS; OR, ENTERTAINMENT FOR INFANT MINDS. First edition, 12mo. *Arliss, etc.,* 1806. Five cuts of children's games.

910 A NOSEGAY, FOR THE TROUBLE OF CULLING; OR, SPORTS OF CHILDHOOD. First edition, sm. 8vo. *Darton,* 1813. With engraved vignette title and 35 engravings of boys playing games.

911 YOUTHFUL SPORTS. First edition, 16mo. [*Darton,* ca. 1815]. With 22 half-page engravings of children's games.

912 FREDERIC AND GEORGE ; OR, THE UTILITY OF PLAY-GROUND SPORTS, AS CONDUCIVE TO HEALTH, HILARITY, AND HARDIHOOD. First edition, 12mo. *Dutton*, [*ca.* 1820]. Two engravings of boys' games.

913 XAVIER LE PRINCE. LES JEUX DES JEUNES GARÇONS, REPRESENTÉS PAR UN GRAND NOMBRE D'ESTAMPES, ACCOMPAGNÉES DE L'EXPLICATION DES RÈGLES, DE FABLES INÉDITÉS ET D'ANECDOTES. First edition, oblong 8vo. [*Paris : Didot*, 1822]. Engraved vignette title and 22 aquatint plates showing boys at play—skittles, fishing, tops, shuttle-cock, tip-cat, solitaire, kites, hop-scotch, paume, etc.

914 HEALTHFUL SPORTS FOR YOUNG LADIES ; ILLUSTRATED BY ELEVEN ELEGANT ENGRAV-INGS, FROM DRAWINGS BY J. DUGOURE, DRAUGHTSMAN TO HIS MAJESTY THE KING OF FRANCE ; ACCOMPANIED BY DESCRIPTIONS TRANSLATED FROM THE FRENCH OF MADE-MOISELLE ST. SERUIN, AND INTERSPERSED WITH ORIGINAL POETRY AND ANECDOTES. First edition, oblong 8vo. *Ackermann*, [1822]. The charming illustrations show young girls playing outdoor games.

915 SCHOOL BOYS' DIVERSIONS : WITH PROPER DIRECTIONS FOR PLAYING THEM ... First edition, sm. 8vo. *Dean and Munday*, [1820]. With folding frontispiece and 2 other plates by R. Stennett.

916 THE STORY OF LITTLE DICK AND HIS PLAY-THINGS ... First edition, 12mo. *Glasgow : Lumsden*, 1823. With 8 full-page woodcuts of children's toys, games, etc.

917 J. ASPIN. ANCIENT CUSTOMS, SPORTS, AND PASTIMES OF THE ENGLISH ... Sm. sq. 8vo. *Harris*, 1832. With 12 full-page hand coloured engravings.

918 THE BOYS' OWN BOOK, OR COMPLETE GUIDE TO ALL THE DIVERSIONS OF YOUTH. *W. Emans*, 1838. Proof pulls of the title and 39 plates, printed four on a sheet, mounted on linen and enclosed in a small portfolio, sm. 4to. These plates show games—indoor and outdoor—experiments, etc.

SECTION II: **INDOOR GAMES**

919 YOUTH'S RECREATION ; OR. MERRY PASTIMES ; IN TWO PARTS ... Sm. 8vo. *For G. Conyers*, 1704. Engraved frontispiece.

920 THE MASQUERADE OR JUBILEE FOR YOUTH CONSISTING OF VARIETY OF CHARACTERS IN PANTOMIME. First edition, 24mo. *Bassam*, [*ca*. 1780]. With engraved title and a frontispiece shewing all the characters in the Masque, including Harlequin, Columbine, The Miser, The Clown, Scaramouch, Pero [*sic*], Punch, Skeleton, Mad Tom, etc. Extremely rare.

920a THE MASQUERADE ... *W. Nicoll*, [*ca*. 1780]. Either this or No. 920 is a copy of the other.

921 THE ART OF TEACHING IN SPORT ; DESIGNED AS A PRELUDE TO A SET OF TOYS ... First edition, fcap. 8vo. *Marshall*, 1785.

922 THE YOUTHFUL JESTER ; OR, REPOSITORY OF WIT AND INNOCENT AMUSEMENT, CONTAINING MORAL AND HUMOUROUS TALES, MERRY JESTS, LAUGHABLE ANECDOTES, AND SMART REPAR-

TEES. First edition, 12mo. *E. Newbery,
ca.* 1789. Not in Welsh. Extremely scarce.
Frontispiece and 12 small cuts.

923 THE MASQUERADE : CONTAINING A VARIETY
OF MERRY CHARACTERS OF ALL SORTS,
PROPERLY DRESSED FOR THE OCCASSION [*sic*].
First edition, 12mo. [*Marshall*], *ca.* 1790.
With numerous woodcuts.

924 A CHOICE COLLECTION OF RIDDLES, CHARADES,
REBUSSES, ETC., BY PETER PUZZLEWELL.
Sm. 8vo. *E. Newbery*, 1794. Welsh, p. 297.
Originally published in 1792.

925 THE YOUTHFUL JESTER ; OR, REPOSITORY OF
WIT AND INNOCENT AMUSEMENT . . . First
edition, 12mo. *E. Newbery*, 1800. Not in
Welsh. (*Cf.* No. 922).

926 THE MAGIC ORACLE ; OR THE AMUSING AND
INSTRUCTIVE TELL-TALE . . . WILL UNERRING-
LY DISCOVER SECRET THOUGHTS ! *Sold at
5, Newgate-Street,* [*ca.* 1800]. Three engraved
cards and sheet of printed instructions, in
original marbled paper slip-case with printed
label, 12mo. The two cards of magic
numbers are coloured, one of these and the
accompanying circle-card fits behind the
other and shows the magic numbers through
an aperture.

927 A NEW RIDDLE BOOK FOR GOOD BOYS AND
GIRLS. First edition, 16mo. *Gainsborough* :
Mozley, 1802. With numerous cuts in the
text.

927a SIXTEEN PUZZLES FOR BOYS AND GIRLS . . .
Darton, ca. 1810. Sixteen coloured pictorial
puzzles. The solutions are given. The
answers to the two shewn are : Gwhelps [*sic*]
and Stile [*sic*].

928 PARLOUR AMUSEMENTS ; OR, A NEW BOOK OF GAMES AND FORFEITS. First edition, 8vo. *Dean and Munday*, [*ca.* 1820]. Folding engraved frontispiece and two other engravings of games, and forfeits. Instructions for 8 games.

929 THE GORDIAN KNOT, A SELECTION OF INGENIOUS PUZZLES ... Sm. 8vo. *Fairburn*, [*ca.* 1820]. With large folding coloured engraving depicting 58 puzzles, among them " Squares in London " and " Places in London."

930 EVENING AMUSEMENTS ; OR, A NEW BOOK OF GAMES AND FORFEITS ; ... WITH FULL AND PLAIN DIRECTIONS FOR CRYING THE FORFEITS, AND NUMEROUS AMUSING AND DIVERTING PENANCES ... First edition, 8vo. *Newman*, [*ca.* 1825]. Coloured engravèd frontispiece " Crying the Forfeits." Gives instructions for eleven indoor games for children.

931 THE GAPING WIDE-MOUTHED, WADDLING FROG. A NEW AND ENTERTAINING GAME OF QUESTIONS AND DEMANDS. First edition, sm. 8vo. *Dean and Munday, etc.*, [1823].

931a ——— FACSIMILE OF THE SAME. *Field & Tuer*, 1887.

932 THE NOBLE, PRANCING, CANTERING HORSE. A NEW GAME OF QUESTIONS AND COMMANDS. First edition, sm. 8vo. *Marshall*, 1821. With coloured title and 14 coloured copperplates.

933 GAMES. HOYLE MADE FAMILIAR ... BY EIDRAH TREBOR [*i.e.* ROBERT HURDIE]. *Ward & Lock, ca.* 1860.

PART X

Board Games

(a) Moral Games.

934 and 934a THE NEW GAME OF HUMAN LIFE. *Wallis & Newbery*, 1790. Plain and coloured examples of the same game. Note the advice to use a " Totum "—" to avoid introducing a Dice Box into private Families."

935 THE NEW GAME OF VIRTUE REWARDED AND VICE PUNISHED. *ca.* 1790. A home-made game, drawn and coloured by hand.

936 VIRTUE REWARDED AND VICE PUNISHED. LAURIE AND WHITTLE'S NEW MORAL AND ENTERTAINING GAME OF THE MANSION OF HAPPINESS. INVENTED BY GEORGE FOX. *Laurie & Whittle*, 1800.

937 A NEW MORAL AND ENTERTAINING GAME OF THE REWARD OF MERIT. INVENTED BY GEORGE FOX . . . *Harris & Whittle*, 1801.

938 THE NEW GAME OF EMULATION : DESIGNED FOR THE AMUSEMENT OF THE YOUTH OF BOTH SEXES, AND CALCULATED TO INSPIRE THEIR MINDS WITH AN ABHORRENCE OF VICE, AND A LOVE OF VIRTUE. *Harris*, 1805. Compare this with No. 939.

939 THE NEW GAME OF EMULATION. *D. Carvalho*, *ca.* 1820. Compare this with No. 938.

940 THE MIRROR OF TRUTH. *Wallis*, 1811.

941 THE ROAD TO THE TEMPLE OF HONOUR AND FAME. *Harris*, 1811.

942 THE COTTAGE OF CONTENT ; OR RIGHT ROADS AND WRONG WAYS. *Spooner*, 1848.

(b) **Animal Games.**

In this section is included the oldest game in the exhibition—the Game of the Goose—and although the earliest examples shewn date from the latter half of the eighteenth century, the game is reputed to have originated in Ancient Greece. The persistence of the original type is remarkable, notably the retention of 63 squares and the marking of a goose on every fifth space. The game appears to be the prototype and origin of every kind of board game from Snakes and Ladders to Race Games.

943 THE ROYAL AND MOST PLEASANT GAME OF THE GOOSE. *Robert Sayer, at the Golden Buck in Fleet Street, ca.* 1770.

944 LE PRIX DE MYTHOLOGIE OU LA MYTHOLOGIE EN JEU D'OIE. MYTHOLOGY IN THE GAME OF THE GOOSE. *Paris,* 1810. A Franco-British version.

945 IL VERO GIUOCO DELL' OCCA. *Milano :* G. *Messugi, ca.* 1820. An Italian version.

946 THE ROYAL GAME OF GOOSE. *ca.* 1840. Note the retention of 63 spaces and the goose emblems.

947 LE PRIX DE SAGESSE OU LA FONTAINE EN JEU. *Paris,* [1810].

948 LA FONTAINE IN THE GAME OF GOOSE. [*Paris*], 1810. This even more strikingly than its French original (No. 947) capitalizes its origin in the Goose game.

949 THE ROYAL PASTIME OF CUPID, OR THE NEW AND MOST PLEASANT GAME OF THE SNAKE. *Robert Sayer, at the Golden Buck ... Fleet Street, ca.* 1770. Another striking derivative from the Goose game.

950 THE NEW GAME OF THE MONKEY. *Wallis, ca.* 1810. From here onwards the variants increase, but the similarity is still remarkable—63 places and " The Inn," " The Well," etc., as obstacles are retained.

951 THE NOBLE GAME OF THE SWAN ... *Darton,* 1821.

952 THE MAJESTIC GAME OF THE ASIATIC OSTRICH. *Darton, ca.* 1821.

953 THE NOBLE GAME OF THE ELEPHANT AND CASTLE. *Darton,* 1822.

954 THE ROYAL GAME OF THE DOLPHIN. *Darton, ca.* 1822.

955 THE HARE AND THE TORTOISE. *Spooner,* 1849. Note the 63 places and the recurrent emblems.

956 DOG TOBY ; OR, MARKET DAY ... 1859.

(c) Race Games.

957 THE ROYAL RACE COURSE. *Madeley, ca.* 1840.

958 THE STEEPLECHASE. *Passmore, ca.* 1850.

959 THE FUNNYSHIRE FOX CHASE. *Spooner, ca.* 1850.

960 THE STEEPLE CHASE. *Spooner,* 1852.

961 THE ROYAL REGATTA. *ca.* 1850.

(d) Miscellaneous Games.

962 THE MAGIC RING. . . . *Champante and Whitrow* 1796.

963 THE NEW GAME OF THE JEW. *Wallis,* 1807.

964 WHO WEARS THE CROWN ? *Wallis, ca.* 1820.

965 and 965a NEW GAME OF GENIUS. *Wallis, ca.* 1825 and 1845. Two similar issues of the same game. Note the difference in the containing slip cases.

966 THE ELEGANT AND INSTRUCTIVE GAME OF USEFUL KNOWLEDGE. *Darton, ca.* 1830.

967 THE CHAPLET OF CHIVALRY OR THE ROYAL TOURNAMENT. *Spooner, ca.* 1835.

968 THE JOURNEY ; OR, CROSS-ROADS TO CONQUEROR'S CASTLE. *Spooner, ca.* 1840.

968a FORTUNIO AND HIS SEVEN GIFTED SERVANTS. *Spooner,* 1846.

969 THE SHAM FIGHT. *Dean, ca.* 1850.

970 GAME OF THE GREAT EXHIBITION OF 1851. *Spooner,* [1851].

971 THE CAUDLE HISTORY. *Wallis, ca.* 1860. A curious repercussion of Jerrold's *Mrs. Caudle.*

972 A COMBINED SOLITAIRE AND " FOX AND GEESE." *Boy's Own Paper, ca.* 1890.

(e) **Juvenile Drama.**

973 REDINGTON'S CHARACTERS AND SCENES IN PAUL CLIFFORD.

974 POLLOCK'S CHARACTERS AND SCENES IN THE WOODMAN'S HUT.

PART XI

Jig-Saw Puzzles

Someone with a turn for etymological and historical research might do worse than attempt the unravelling of the origin and history of jig-saw puzzles. He might start with the name. The earliest specimens were almost exclusively educational and they are interesting and successful examples of an early endeavour to introduce play-methods into an educational curriculum.

No example earlier than about 1770 is known to me and the earliest are invariably geographical. They were then called " Dissected Maps " and it seems significant that for several years they were produced exclusively by the firm of Wallis, expert cartographers and famous map-makers.

No. 987 is a dissected map published in about 1880, which makes it clear that this name for these toys persisted until then and by the turn of the century, while they were then called Puzzles, this had not yet become Jig-saw Puzzle.

This is extremely odd because the New Oxford Dictionary (V. 581, 1901), in defining " jig-saw " quotes from Richards, *Wood-working Factories*, 1873, to the effect that the tool was then generally superseded. It would be interesting to know how the name of the implement came to be tacked on adjectivally to an eighteenth-century invention more than thirty years after the tool itself had gone out of use.

The jig-saw appears to have given way to the

fret-saw, yet there is no trace of the toys ever having been called fret-saw puzzles, which is probably a more accurate reference to the way they were made at the time when they acquired their modern description.

Equally deep is the mystery surrounding the identity of their inventor. That the firm of Wallis first put these puzzles on the market seems almost certain, but whether the notion was evolved by an employee, by an outsider, or, as I like to think by E. Wallis, a junior member of the firm who later enlarged the firm's juvenile list considerably, it is impossible to say. But there is the double problem stated for the benefit of anyone who cares to attempt its solution.

The evolution of the puzzle is evident from the examples shewn. No. 976 shews the kind of " dissected map " of which all the very earliest examples consist. No. 975 shows an early experiment with non-geographical subjects, but it is not until well into the nineteenth century that a single large picture is comprised in a dissected puzzle.

975 DISSECTED TABLES OF ROMAN HISTORY CHRONOLOGICALLY ARRANGED. *Newbery & Wallis, Oct.* 12*th,* 1789. An early attempt to get away from maps as a subject for jig-saw puzzles. Judging by its lack of emulators, it was not a success.

976 WALLIS'S NEW DISSECTED MAP OF IRELAND ENGRAVED FROM THE LATEST AUTHORITIES FOR THE USE OF YOUNG STUDENTS IN GEOGRAPHY. *J. Wallis,* [1796].

977 ENGLAND AND WALES DISSECTED ON THE BEST PRINCIPLES FOR TEACHING GEOGRAPHY. *ca.* 1800.

978 A NEW MAP OF THE POST ROADS OF SCOTLAND. *London : E. Wallis ; Sidmouth : J. Wallis, ca.* 1810.

979 THE HISTORY OF ENGLAND. *ca.* 1810.

980 GAME OF THE STAR-SPANGLED BANNER, OR EMIGRANTS TO THE UNITED STATES. *E. Wallis, ca.* 1835. One of the handsomest and most complicated puzzles of any period.

981 THE AERIAL TRANSIT COMPANY'S STATION IN THE PLAINS OF HINDOSTAN. *Madeley, lith., ca.* 1843. This very remarkable jig-saw is one of the numerous publicity stunts evolved from the fertile brain of Henson, whose " aerostat " invented in company with Stringfellow, is said to have been the first heavier than air machine capable of flight. Although it never advanced beyond a working model Henson had grandiose ideas of its prospects, formed a company to exploit it, and published prints, silk-handkerchiefs and broadsides, with views of his machine in full flight. The two representations of the machine shewn in the puzzle indicate its striking likeness to the monoplane used by Latham in his abortive attempts to fly the English Channel some sixty years later.

982 EUROPE DELINEATED. A GEOGRAPHICAL GAME AND DISSECTED PUZZLE. *John Betts, ca.* 1845. An ingenious combination of cartography and pictures.

983 NEW DOUBLE PUZZLE. RAILWAY SCENES. *Philip and Son, ca.* 1850. An early example of a double puzzle, on the back of the picture-puzzle is a map of England and Wales—equal proportions of jam and powder.

984 THE HISTORY OF MOSES. *William Spooner, ca.* 1855. A very superior puzzle mounted on mahogany.

985 ZOOLOGICAL GARDENS. *ca.* 1860.

986 HAWTHORN FARM, WITH HORSES, COWS, SHEEP, PIGS, GEESE, DUCKS, FOWLS, AND OTHER THINGS. *ca.* 1860.

987 ESLICK'S PATENT DISSECTED MAP OF RUSSIA IN EUROPE, DESIGNED EXPRESSLY TO IMPRESS UPON THE MINDS OF CHILDREN THE EXACT SHAPE AND POSITION OF EACH COUNTY. *Philip Son & Nephew, ca.,* 1880.

988 THE ARMY PUZZLE BOX. *ca.* 1900. Four puzzles in one box. There were a whole series of these, each devoted to a different subject—the Navy, the Railways, etc.

PART XII

Peep-Shows

Little or nothing appears to be known of the origin of what is now known as the peep-show. Strictly speaking the peep-show of earlier days was a much more elaborate affair and was invariably home made. It was contained in a large box with one or more peep-holes and was wheeled about from place to place by the owner who charged a small fee for a peep at the wonders within. These varied, sometimes being a panoramic view of a city, landscape, or battle, and sometimes a fairy play or a drama. The display was made up of cut-out scenes and figures very similar in kind to the minature versions shewn here and similarly dependent on the maker's ingenuity for the illusion of perspective.

These peep-shows or galanty shows were common in the eighteenth century but it was not before about 1825 that some now unknown genius conceived the idea of simplification and reduction of scale which resulted in the enormously popular " Perspective View," " Areaorama," " Regiaorama," as they were variously called. The early subjects were varied, including views of Regent's and St. James's Parks, theatre scenes, military reviews, etc., but the idea does not seem to have caught on until Brunel started his Thames Tunnel.

Some idea of the sensation caused by this unusual engineering feat may be gathered from the fact that the present writer's collection comprises seventy-five peep-shows, of which twenty-three are of The Tunnel. These Tunnel peep-shows were made long before it was finished ; after the opening ceremony stalls were rented for the sale of souvenirs and one of the most enterprising vendors, Azulay by name, sold rather simple and crude peep-shows of the Tunnel inself, the covers of which were usually made of cloth stripped from small books.

The Great Exhibition of 1851 revived the interest in these pretty toys and nearly twenty different versions of this great show are known.

The peep-show seems to have been a British invention and the earliest ones are usually the best. The Germans, with their onslaught on the British juvenile market in the 1830's copied, cheapened and coarsened the thing, but the later French ones are the daintiest of all.

In modern times the toy has been occasionally revived for advertising purposes.

989 THE AERAORAMA.   A VIEW IN REGENT'S PARK. *S. & J. Fuller, May 1st*, 1825.

990 DAS RHEINTHAL VON BINGEN BIS ZUM LURLEY. *ca.* 1830.

991 THE TUNNEL.   *T. Brown, June 16th*, 1825.

992 THE TUNNEL.   PONT SOUS LA TAMISE. [*Paris*], *ca.* 1826.

993 DER TUNNEL.   *ca.* 1830. An elaborate version with three peep-holes, intended to convey an impression of the under-water nature of the Tunnel.

994 A VIEW OF THE TUNNEL UNDER THE THAMES AS IT WILL APPEAR WHEN COMPLETED. *M. Gouyn, Aug.* 3, 1829.

995 LANE'S TELESCOPIC VIEW OF THE INTERIOR OF THE GREAT INDUSTRIAL EXHIBITION. *C. Lane, June 3rd,* 1851.

996 LANE'S TELESCOPIC VIEW OF THE CEREMONY OF THE OPENING OF THE GREAT EXHIBITION OF ALL NATIONS, 1851. *C. A. Lane, 15th August,* 1851.

997 THE GREAT EXHIBITION OF INDUSTRY. 1851. A rather crude foreign version, probably German, with a tri-lingual title—the French title is a little shaky.

PART XIII

Four Publishers'
Catalogues

998 LAURIE AND WHITTLE'S CATALOGUE OF NEW AND INTERESTING PRINTS CONSISTING OF ENGRAVINGS, METZOTINTOS, ETC. . . . *Printed and Published by Robert Laurie and James Whittle* . . . 8vo. 1795. This extensive catalogue, which was the subject of an article in *The Connoisseur*, December, 1945, includes Writing Sheets, Harlequinades, Jig-saws, and many other things featured in the present exhibition.

999 WALLIS'S CATALOGUE OF AMUSING PUBLICATIONS FOR THE IMPROVEMENT OF YOUTH ; *Sold at the Dissected Map Factory and Instructive Repository, No. 42, Skinner Street, Snowhill* . . . 1813. Note the obvious popularity of jig-saws, deducible from their prominence on the title-page of this catalogue. Many of the games and books exhibited here are listed in this catalogue.

1000 CATALOGUE OF MAPS, ATLASES, DISSECTED MAPS, AMUSING, INSTRUCTIVE AND EDUCATIONAL GAMES, ETC., ETC. *Published by John Betts*, [*ca.* 1850]. Note that jig-saws are still called " Dissected Maps."

1001 ONE HUNDRED THINGS WORTH KNOWING. A DESCRIPTIVE LIST OF THE BEST GAMES . . . *H. G. Clarke & Co.*, *ca.* 1900. This consists mostly of conjuring tricks, but juvenile theatres and dramas for use in them are included. They consisted of old stock taken from Webb and Redington.